NETWORKING

STEVE RACKLEY

In easy steps is an imprint of Computer Step
Southfield Road . Southam
Warwickshire CV47 0FB . United Kingdom
www.ineasysteps.com

Notice of Liability

Every effort has been made to ensure that this book contains accurate and current information. However, Computer Step and the author shall not be liable for any loss or damage suffered by readers as a result of any information contained herein.

Acknowledgements and Trademarks

Product images courtesy of Sony Corp., Samsung Electronics, Philips Consumer Electronics, Palm Inc., D-Link Systems Inc., Cisco Systems Inc. (including Linksys), Buffalo Technology Inc. and Belkin Components Ltd.

All trademarks are acknowledged as belonging to their respective companies.

Printed and bound in the United Kingdom

ISBN 1-84078-170-X

Contents

Introduction to Networking

In this introductory chapter we'll take a look, if you're not already convinced, at why networking is set to become as common in the home of the future as the TV is in today's home.

We'll look at the main reasons you might have for starting out on networking and at the ease and advantages of going wireless (as well as some of the current limitations). A quick look under the hood will either whet your appetite to learn more about the inner workings of networks or leave you simply in awe that these things work at all!

Finally we'll map out the key steps that will be covered in later chapters as you build and develop your network and your knowledge of networking.

Covers

Chapter One

Who Needs a Network?

The computer in some shape or form, whether it's the desktop workhorse, a laptop, notebook or PDA, or even a computer games box, is fast becoming as common around the home as other appliances like TVs or Hi-Fi systems.

Gone are the days when the family's sole PC took an honored place in the corner of the den or study; now they're also in the kids bedrooms, for homework as well as games.

There may be a queue to use the main desktop machine too, for email, Internet surfing and the like, and it's even more of a bottleneck because it runs the printer, scanner and other gear as well as the Internet connection.

And on the horizon we've got Hi-Fi with PC connections and new media streamers that will be able to serve your video and music collections up to you wherever you are in the home.

Enter the Network

A home network can also give a new lease of life to the old PC you were about to recycle. It may not have the speed but it will be able to share resources like mass storage or the DVD-RW with your latest hot machine.

Into this increasingly complex scene comes networking, a solution that delivers easy shared access to all the household's IT resources, and a new level of family harmony! No more the happy frustration of waiting for the kids' homework to be done before you can check your email.

A network will allow every computer in your home to access the Internet connection, printer and other resources. You'll be able to open up files on one machine from another and share storage devices such as hard drives or DVD-ROMs.

In a small office environment, sharing files and mass storage among staff, as well as reducing the number of printers around the office, can give a rapid payback to the modest investment of time and money needed to get started with networking.

Networking in Windows XP

Windows XP has been designed with networking in mind, and takes a lot of the hard work out of setting up your network, whether wired or wireless. Networking is now a realistic option for the average home or small office user, without the need for the skills of an IT professional.

Why Go Wireless?

If you're just starting out with networking, or if you already have a wired network and want to extend the reach to new areas of your home or office, then it's a good time to think about going wireless.

The key standards are 802.11b, also known as Wi-Fi, and 802.11g. See chapter 13 to learn more on the meaning of these terms.

Wireless networking has taken off in the last few years as a result of the ratification of standards from the IEEE (Institute of Electrical and Electronics Engineers) that ensure interoperability of equipment from different manufacturers.

Coupled with this there have been dramatic price reductions on the chip sets that drive wireless hardware and, particularly in the UK and Europe, decreasing regulation of the spectrum used for wireless networking.

Wireless advantages

In the home, going wireless has two main advantages, both of which are pretty obvious. Firstly you don't need to hassle with cables, so wireless is a lot more partner friendly than wired networking!

Security is an issue that will need your attention if you go wireless rather than wired. We cover the key security issues in later chapters.

No need to drill holes through walls for cables and sockets. No crouching in dusty loft spaces laying cable runs out of sight, or time spent redecorating after all of the above.

Second advantage is the total flexibility of wireless – you'll not be tied down to the locations you initially decided to wire up. If you want to install a new computer in another room you can leave the toolbox in the garage. If you have a mobile computer you can also move out of doors and check your email with your feet up in an easy chair on the lawn.

Rise of the mobile worker

The same advantages of wireless flexibility apply from the standpoint of running a small office network too. Also, if any of your work force spends a lot of time out of the office, then equipping them with wireless networking capability will allow them to keep in touch through the growing network of wireless hotspots.

Hotspots are covered in detail in chapter 4.

What Makes a Network Work?

At first sight, sharing information and other resources between computers might seem like a fairly simple task. Computers all store information in binary form, so if you make sure the devices all understand that code then you just need to connect the wires together, right?

Of course it is that simple if you just want to plug a printer or scanner into a computer. Then the device driver ensures that both ends are speaking the same digital language.

Unfortunately it's not quite that simple and once you get a little insight into the seemingly simple act of sending and receiving an email you may be amazed that it works at all.

The best way to get a quick idea about how a network works is to take a look at the OSI model that's used worldwide as a guideline for developing the standards that enable networking.

The OSI network model

The Open Systems Interconnect (OSI) model was developed by the International Standards Organization (ISO) to provide a guideline for hardware and software developers who were producing standards for networking computing devices.

The model divides up the networking problem into seven so called "layers" of related tasks.

7; Application layer	Standards to define the provision of services to application, such as checking resource availability, authenticating users, etc.
6; Presentation layer	Standards to control the translation of incoming and outgoing data from one presentation format to another.
5; Session layer	Standards to manage communication between the sending and receiving computers. This communication is achieved by establishing and managing "sessions".
4; Transport layer	Standards to ensure reliable completion of data transfers, covering error recovery, data flow control, etc. Makes sure all data packets have arrived.
3; Network layer	Standards to define the management of network connections, routing, relaying and terminating connections between nodes in the network.
2; Data link layer	Standards to specify the way in which devices access and share the transmission medium and ensure reliability of the physical connection.
1; Physical layer	Standards to control transmission of the data stream over a particular medium, at the level of voltages, signal durations and frequencies.

A protocol is a standard set of definitions and rules that specify how each layer will operate and cooperate with the other layers in the model.

Standards or protocols are defined for each layer to ensure interoperability of hardware and software.

Sending an email

An example will show how these layers combine to achieve a task such as sending an email between two computers. Rita, sending an email to Rick, types her message into an email application such as MS Outlook.

When she presses "Send", the operating system combines her message with a set of application layer (Layer 7) instructions that will eventually be read and actioned by the corresponding application layer in the operating system on Rick's computer.

HTTP is an example of a protocol operating at levels 6 and 7.

The message plus instructions is passed to the part of Rita's operating system that deals with presentation tasks like encryption, and a new set of instructions are added to the message.

Ethernet and Wi-Fi are examples of standards for the physical and data link layers.

This process continues down through the successive layers, with the message gathering instructions at each level. On the Transport Layer, Rita's message will be broken down into smaller data packets with each one transmitted separately.

At the Physical Layer, the standards determine how the signals will be sent in terms of voltages and frequencies.

Receiving an email

On arrival at Rick's computer, the Layer 1 instructions will be executed, stripped off the message, and the remaining message plus instructions passed up to the components dealing with the Data Link tasks at Layer 2 in Rick's system.

TCP is one of the most important protocols that deals with these transport issues.

Again this process is repeated up through software layers. Again at the Transport Layer, the software will ensure that all data packets making up the message are received and will provide error recovery if any have gone missing.

Finally Rick's email application will receive and display the characters that make up Rita's original message.

So, things are pretty complex under the hood, but thankfully you don't need to deal with this complexity with today's hardware and software. You'll find that getting your network up and running smoothly is just a few easy steps away.

Key Stages in Developing Your Network

Later chapters are arranged to take you progressively through the key stages of building and expanding a network and building up your knowledge of networking along the way. Of course if there's one topic you want to start on, perhaps mobile networking at Wi-Fi hotspots, then jump right in there.

If not, here is the outline of how the topics will develop and build on each other as we progress through chapters 2 to 9:

USB stands for Universal Serial Bus. See chapter 13 for a guide to all the networking alphabet soup!

2 We start in chapter 2 by taking a look at wired networking, first using simple USB connections and then using the Ethernet.

3 Next we'll cover the basic aspects of networking in Windows XP, setting up a network and sharing resources.

4 Chapter 4 will get you started on wireless networking, wireless enabling a laptop and signing on at a Wi-Fi hotspot.

Ad hoc mode is the simplest of the two modes that can be used for making wireless network connections.

5 Then you'll learn how to set up your first wireless network, using ad hoc mode to make a connection between two computers.

6 Next we look at advanced network options under Windows XP, Internet sharing, firewalls, and monitoring network performance.

7 Chapter 7 will help you set up a more advanced wireless network using infrastructure mode.

Consider chapter 8 as mandatory reading once your network's up and running.

8 Security is the next topic we'll cover, with particular emphasis on issues for wireless networking.

9 Extending wireless network range will be discussed next, including antennas, community wireless and setting up a WISP.

We'll continue with a chapter on troubleshooting, plus a look at what the future might hold in store for home and small office networking, and conclude with a chapter covering online sources of further information and an explanation of the key abbreviations and technical terms you'll come across as you take your first steps in networking.

Wired Networking Basics

In this chapter, after taking a quick look at what can be achieved using your existing USB connections to link computers and peripherals, you'll learn the basics of setting up a wired Ethernet network.

We start by taking a quick look at network protocols and topologies, then look at typical wired network components. Finally we look at installing and configuring a network adapter card and wiring up the network.

Covers

Chapter Two

Making the Most of USB

The Universal Serial Bus (USB) connections which are included on virtually all computers manufactured today are often overlooked as a means of achieving a simple networking capability.

These components are available for USB 1.1 speeds of 8Mbps, close to the 10Mbps of a 10Base Ethernet network, or for USB 2.0 data rates of 480Mbps.

USB networking components allow you to link two or more computers for file sharing, as well as allowing multiple computers to connect to resources such as printers and modems.

The catch is that you don't get the full network flexibility that you would with an Ethernet network that we'll look at next. For example, when sharing a printer you need to manually select which computer is "active" and has access to the printer.

USB Network Components

USB connecting cables have a flat type A connection at one end to plug into the computer and a more square shaped type B connector at the other end to plug into the USB device.

Port Selection Button

A USB 4-Port switch like the Belkin F1U200 allows you to connect four computers to a shared peripheral such as a printer. The front button manually switches between computers.

The Direct Connect device also allows you to connect more computers in a daisy chain or a tree structure. TCP/IP is supported so that data can be addressed to a specific destination.

Belkin F5U104 Direct Connect allows you to directly link two computers through their USB ports for file, peripheral or drive sharing, or for network games.

Protocols and Packets

While USB can give you a degree of file and device sharing, to get the full benefit of networking you need to go to the next level. This means using the full capabilities of the OSI network model and the standards like Ethernet and Wi-Fi that have been developed in accordance with the model.

We'll learn in this chapter that it actually isn't that difficult to set up a network, but this fact is a testament to over thirty years of effort by thousands of computer scientists who figured out how to make it all work.

A major part of that effort was in establishing the standard languages (or protocols) that would ensure computers would understand each other when they try to communicate.

For wired networks, the key standard goes by the useful designation "IEEE 802.3", having been developed by the Institute of Electrical and Electronics Engineers (IEEE). It's more generally known as Ethernet.

This standard deals with such things as allowable data rates and how data is encoded, specifications for the interconnecting medium (cables or optical fibres) and how to avoid data logjams when several devices try to talk at the same time.

This process is managed by other network protocols such as TCP/IP.

A key to making networks work is breaking up the data to be transmitted into smaller "packets", transmitting these packets independently and then reassembling them to rebuild the complete message at the destination.

Here's what a data packet on an Ethernet network looks like when it's put into a "frame" for transmission:

Preamble	Destination	Source	Type	Data	Check
Tells the network that this is a frame	Where this frame is going to	Where this frame has come from	What to do with the data on arrival	The actual data packet	To check the frame is undamaged
8 bytes long	6 bytes long	6 bytes long	2 bytes long	46 to 1500 bytes long	4 bytes long

Network Topologies

Network topology relates to the geometry of the device interconnections in your network. There are two main network topologies that are relevant for home or small office networking, bus and star, and a number of others that are used in large scale corporate networks that we'll not touch on here.

Bus topology

In a bus topology all networked devices are connected to a single interconnecting medium called the bus.

In a bus network the available bandwidth is shared by all devices. When one computer is transmitting data all the others have to wait their turn.

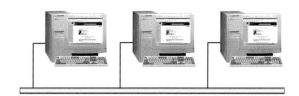

This topology has the advantages of cheapness and simplicity. No additional hardware is required beyond network adapters in each device and installation requires a single cable lay to each device location.

Star topology

The pros and cons of hubs and switches are discussed on page 18.

In a star topology each device is connected through a dedicated cable to a central point, where an additional network device called a hub or switch is located. The hub or switch controls the flow of data packets from one device to another across the network.

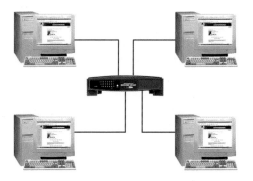

Wired Network Components

The terms network adapter, interface card or NIC are all synonymous.

The key component that is required by every computer or other device that will be connected to the network is a Network Interface Card (NIC) or network adapter.

NICs come in a wide variety of shapes and sizes, designed to connect desktop computers, laptops, PDAs or other devices to the network.

Network Interface Cards (NICs)

If you want to avoid getting the screwdriver out, you can also get a NIC that plugs into a USB port on your desktop computer.

The Belkin F5D5000u is a typical NIC for a desktop computer, fitting into a spare PCI slot.

You may see NICs with other types of connectors, but the RJ45 plug is the most common.

RJ45 Ethernet socket

Some of the features of PCI adapters you may want to look out for when selecting your gear are:

Wake-on-LAN, allows a computer hosting shared resources such as a printer to be awakened from sleep mode by a signal sent from another computer in the network.

Flow Control, allows data transmission to be paused if high traffic on a network switch is causing the data buffer to fill up.

Full Duplex Data Transfer, allows data transmission and reception at the same time, speeding-up high bandwidth applications like network games.

10/100Base-T, supports Fast Ethernet data transfer at 100Mbps as well as standard Ethernet at 10Mbps.

For laptop computers, the interface card plugs into a PC (PCMCIA) slot. Various types are available with either an integral RJ45 socket, such as the D-Link DFE 670TXD, or else allow the Ethernet cable to connect to the RJ45 socket on a "dongle", like the Belkin F5D5020u.

Check your computer before you rush out to buy your interface cards. Laptops in particular are increasingly being shipped network ready, with a network interface pre-installed.

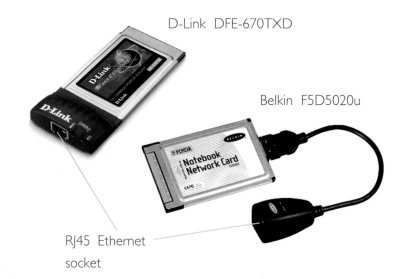

D-Link DFE-670TXD

Belkin F5D5020u

RJ45 Ethernet socket

As we saw in the last section, for a bus topology all the hardware you need is a NIC for each networked device. The next step up in network complexity uses a hub or switch to drive a network wired up in a star topology.

Hubs, Switches and Routers

Hubs are central units that connect through individual cables to each network computer or other device. The key feature of a hub is that it shares the available bandwidth between all devices on the network.

In fact, the network traffic will be a mix of data packets from the two transmitting computers. This is why the data frame structure (page 15) and protocols such as TCP are needed to make sure the messages get put back together correctly.

This means that if two computers want to transmit data at the same time the overall transfer speed will be reduced. The full network bandwidth can be made available to every transmitting device if a switch is used instead of a hub.

A switch receives incoming frames from multiple sources at once, reads the destination address in each frame (see page 15) and only transmits the frame on to the intended destination.

A switch clearly needs more computing power and storage space, and the hub therefore has the advantage on cost. For most home networking applications a hub will be a good choice, but if response time is important and bandwidth is at a premium, for example to play games over the network, then you'll want a switch.

If you need more ports to expand your network, hubs and switches can be cascaded by connecting them together through one of the ports.

The D-Link DE-805TP is a typical Ethernet hub for home or small office networks, with 5 ports running at 10Mbps. An LED on the front panel indicates activity on each port.

Ethernet switches like the D-Link DSS-8+ generally offer both 10Mbps and Fast Ethernet at 100Mbps.

If you're going to be sharing a broadband Internet connection then you'll also need a router to control traffic between your network computers and the Internet. Options are a stand alone router to connect up to your hub or switch, or alternatively a combined switch/router.

Installing a Network Interface Card and Drivers

Any computer that you want to connect to your network that does not have a network interface card already will need to have one installed and configured. Follow these steps for each computer.

Installing the Network Interface Card

To protect the card from static electricity, touch a metal part of the computer chassis before unwrapping the card to make sure that any static has been discharged to earth.

1. Switch off the computer, unplug the power cord and remove the back cover or outer case.

2. Locate a spare PCI slot and remove the slot cover plate by unscrewing the securing screw.

3. Carefully but firmly press the card into the connector on the motherboard. Secure the card to the computer chassis with the securing screw.

4. Replace the computer's back cover or outer case.

You are now ready to install the drivers for the network interface card that will enable your computer to access the new hardware.

Automatic NIC Driver Installation

1. Plug in the power cord and switch on the computer.

2. Windows XP should automatically detect and identify the new hardware.

The red X beside the network icon indicates that this network connection is not available.

3. If drivers are available on your computer these will be automatically installed and the new hardware will be ready for operation.

An icon to indicate the new network connection will appear in the notification area.

It will save you a few clicks if you put a shortcut to Network Connections on your desktop. Click Start, Control Panel. Right click Network Connections and select Create Shortcut. Click Yes to put the shortcut on your desktop.

4 You can also check the status of the network connection by clicking Start, Control Panel, Network Connections. The Network Connections window will open and indicate the status of your LAN connection.

If Windows XP is not able to find the drivers for your Network Interface card, you will have to manually install the drivers from the installation CD provided by your hardware manufacturer.

Manually Installing NIC Drivers

If you don't see System in the Control Panel then switch to Classic View in the Task Panel on the left of the Control Panel dialog box.

1 Click Start, Control Panel, System, and select the Hardware tab on the System Properties dialog.

2 Click the Add Hardware Wizard button.

3 The Add Hardware Wizard will search for the new hardware installed in your computer.

4 When prompted by the Add Hardware Wizard, navigate to the appropriate folder on your installation CD and select the driver for your network interface card.

5 To check the installation, click the Device Manager button on the System Properties dialog box, scroll down to Network Adapters and you will see the driver you have just installed.

Wiring Up Your Network

Now that you've decided on your network topology and selected and installed your hardware components you're ready to wire up and start networking.

Computer to computer connection

A crossover is a cable in which, rather than going straight through (pin 1 to pin 1, 2 to 2, etc.) the transmit pins (1 & 2) at one end are connected to receive pins (3 & 6) at the other end, and vice versa.

To create a simple peer-to-peer connection between two computers all you'll need is a single crossover cable.

Plug this cable into the two NICs and turn to the next chapter where you'll find out how to set up your network under Windows XP.

Connecting a hub, switch or router

If your network will be using a hub, switch or router to connect a number of computers or other devices, you'll need a network cable for each connection. Connect each device up to your hub, switch or router.

The RJ45 jack shown here is the standard BaseT Ethernet connector.

If you're going to share broadband Internet, one connection on your router will be dedicated to your cable or DSL modem. This may be labeled Internet, Modem or WAN.

Any type of like-to-like connection will require a crossover cable. This could be hub-to-hub as well as computer-to-computer. Some hardware auto detects the type of connection and reconfigures itself, avoiding the need for crossover cables. Check your hardware manual if in doubt.

With a larger network you may be cascading hubs or switches to give yourself more ports to work with. Your hardware may come with an uplink port that is specially configured for this type of connection. Otherwise you'll need to make these hub-to-hub or switch-to-switch connections using crossover cables.

Network Resource Sharing

Windows XP is designed to allow you to share a wide range of resources across your network, everything from pictures and music files to a printer, scanner or hard drive.

In this chapter you'll learn how to set up a network using Windows XP and then how to enable your resources for sharing with other computers on your network.

Covers

Chapter Three

Network Setup Using Windows XP

You will need to complete this network setup routine whether your network is wired or wireless.

Once your network adapter cards are installed and running in the computers that you want to network together, the Windows XP Network Setup Wizard will quickly take you through the steps to ensure that the necessary networking software components are installed and configured to enable the network connection.

1 Click Start, Settings, Network Connections or Start, Settings, Control Panel, Network Connections.

2 In the left hand Task Pane, select Set up a home or small office network.

3 Click Next to start setting up the network connection.

More on Internet connection sharing and Internet connection firewall in chapter 6.

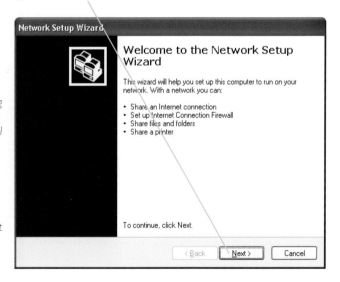

Read the checklist for creating a network and the linked networking overview if you would like more background info on Windows networking.

4 At each of the Wizard dialog boxes that follow make your choice and click Next.

5 If the computer you are setting up connects to the Internet indicate how this is done.

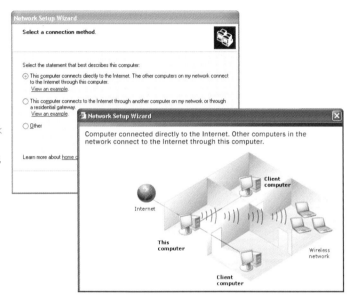

An ad hoc network may not have an Internet connection, in which case select Other here and This computer belongs to a network that does not have an Internet connection in the following dialog box. Sharing your Internet connection is covered in more detail in chapter 6.

6 If the Wizard finds several connections on your computer you will be asked to select the one that connects to the Internet.

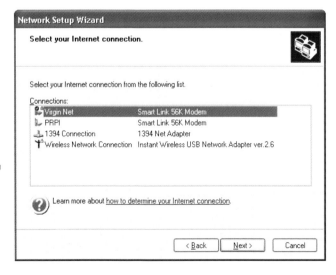

If in doubt, read the information on the Learn More link.

7 When several connections are found, the Wizard can determine for you which connections to use for linking to other computers, for example if your network has wired and wireless segments.

If your network has both wired and wireless links, network bridging will enable your wireless networked computers to access devices such as a DV camera linked to your main computer by Firewire (IEEE 1394). Follow the link to learn more about bridging.

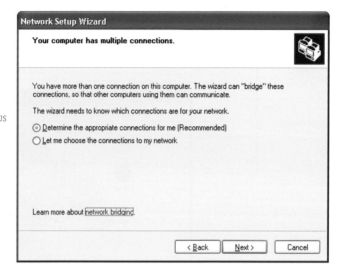

8 Specify a description and name for your computer so that it can be uniquely identified in the network.

You can also change the computer or workgroup name by clicking Start, Settings, Control Panel, System, Computer Name, Change.

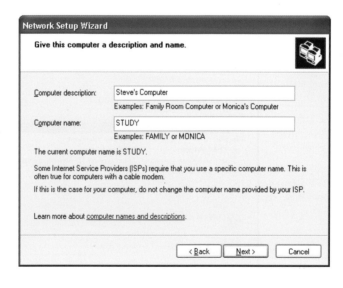

9 Specify a Workgroup name for your network.

Computers in your network must each have different computer names but must all have the same workgroup name.

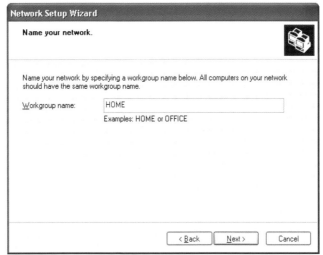

10 Make sure your settings are correct and then click Next. If any of the settings need to be changed click Back to the appropriate dialog box and make the necessary changes.

Your settings will be different from those shown here.

11 Windows will then configure your computer for networking. Once completed, create a Network Setup Disk to configure the other computers you'll be using in your network.

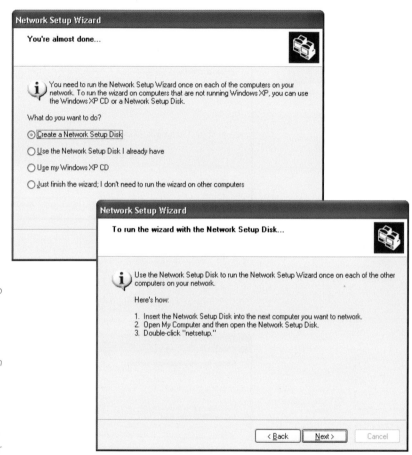

To run the netsetup program on your other computers navigate to the Setup Disk using My Computer and double click on the netsetup application.

Remember the workgroup name must be the same for every computer in your network.

12 Click Finish and your first computer will be successfully set up for networking.

13 Run the netsetup program from the Network Setup Disk on each of the other computers you'll be using in your network. When that's complete you'll be ready to start sharing resources between computers in your network.

Sharing Files and Folders

Folders are the resources that you are likely to be sharing most often across your network. For a file to be shared it has to reside within a folder that has been set up for sharing.

Follow these steps to share a folder.

1 Right click on the folder you wish to share and select Sharing and Security from the drop down menu.

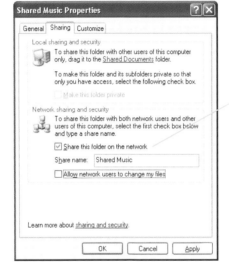

2 Select Share this folder on the network, and enter a Share name by which the folder will be identified on the network. The Share name does not have to be the same as the original folder name.

3 If you want other users to be able to change your files as well as to read them, then check the Allow network users to change my files checkbox.

4 The folder is now shared. The small hand that appears below the file icon indicates that it is shared with other network users.

Shared Music

Moving or renaming shared folders

If you try to move or rename a shared folder you will get a warning that the folder will no longer be shared after it has been renamed or moved.

Private folders

If the options on the Sharing tab are inactive, it is because the folder you are trying to share resides within another folder that has been designated as a private folder. Move the folder you want to share out of the private folder or change the parent folder so that it is no longer private.

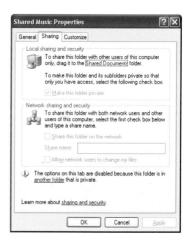

You can prevent other network users from accessing a sub-folder within a shared folder by making the sub-folder private.

1 Right click the sub-folder you want to protect, and select Security and Sharing.

2 Select the Make this folder private check box and click Apply.

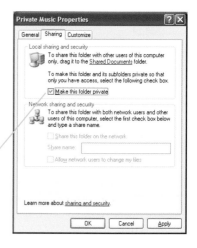

Sharing a Printer

Sharing a printer with other users on your network is a two stage process. First the printer needs to be enabled for sharing on the computer that hosts the printer connection, and then the network printer needs to be set up on the other computers that want to print to it.

Enabling a printer for sharing

1 On the computer that the printer is connected to, access the printer by clicking Start, Control Panel, Printers and Faxes.

2 Right-click the printer that you want to share and click on Sharing...

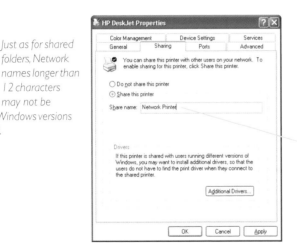

Just as for shared folders, Network names longer than 12 characters may not be recognized by Windows versions earlier than XP.

3 Select Share this printer and enter a Share name. This is the name that will identify the printer to all network users.

If Windows XP does not have a suitable printer driver you will be asked to specify the location of the driver. You may need to find this from your printer manufacturer's website.

4 If any of the other computers that will use the shared printer are running older versions of Windows, Windows XP allows you to keep the printer drivers on the computer that maintains the shared printer. Click Advanced and indicate the additional drivers you need to install.

5 A small hand appears below the printer icon to confirm that it is now available for sharing.

Setting up a network printer

1 On each of the other networked computers in turn, click Start, Control Panel, Printers and Faxes, and select Add a printer from the Printer Tasks list.

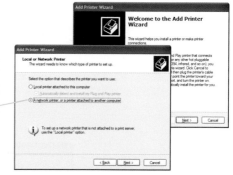

2 The Add Printer Wizard will start. Click Next and on the next screen select A network printer. Click Next again.

3 Select Browse for Printer and click Next.

If the wizard only shows the workgroup but no printers, click on the workgroup icon to show computers, and then on the computer icon to show shared printers.

4 The wizard will identify other computers in the workgroup and list shared printers.

5 Select the printer that you want to add and click Next. You will be asked whether you want this to be your default printer.

Sharing a Drive

As well as sharing folders and printers, you can share a complete drive, such as your hard drive, with other users on your network.

Although this might seem like an easy way to avoid having to set up sharing for a number of different folders, there is a risk in giving other users access to your main drive. A careless user could delete important system files and make your computer inoperable.

However, sharing a secondary drive, such as a CD-RW, may be useful if other computers on your network don't have this type of drive installed.

Enabling a drive for sharing

1 Click Start, My Computer and right click the drive you want to share.

2 Click Sharing and Security.

3 Click the If you understand the risk but still want to share... link to continue to set up sharing for this drive.

The Sharing options tab for a drive is identical to the tab for a folder.

The limit of 12 characters for Share names also applies here if you want to be able to access the shared drive from computers running pre-XP versions of Windows.

4   Select Share this folder on the network, and enter a Share name.

5   The familiar hand will appear beneath the drive icon to show that it is now shared on the network.

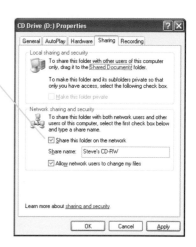

CD Drive (D:)

Mapping a shared drive

If you are going to access a shared drive frequently from another computer you can "map" the drive so that it appears in My Computer on the networked computer as if it was a local drive on that computer.

You can map a folder as well as a complete drive in the same way.

1   Open My Computer, right click in the Toolbar and select Customize.

2   Select Map Drive from the list of buttons here and click Add.

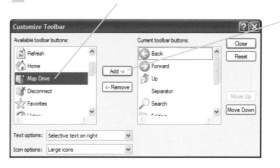

3   Select and Add the Disconnect toolbar button. Click Close.

4   To map a network drive click the new Map Drive button on your My Computer toolbar.

Map Drive

5 Select a drive letter from the drop down list of available unassigned letters and use the Browse button to locate the drive or folder that you want to map to that drive letter.

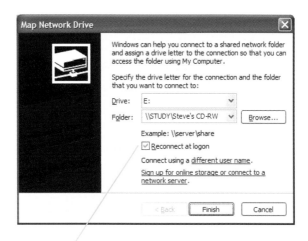

6 If you want Windows to connect to the drive each time you start up select the Reconnect at logon check box. Click Finish.

7 On the networked computer in My Computer the mapped drive will now appear alongside your local drive. The icon shows a cable beneath the drive to indicate that it is a network resource rather than a local drive.

My Network Places

Now that your network is set up and a number of folders and devices have been enabled for sharing with other computers, you can use My Network Places to locate the shared resources and connect to information on the other computers.

If you will be using shared resources quite often it's useful to put a shortcut to My Network Places on your desktop.

Click Start, My Network Places, or if My Network Places does not appear in your Start Menu click Start, My Computer and then select My Network Places from the Other Places list in the Task pane.

The computer that holds the shared folder or device must be switched on before you can access it. Windows will warn you if the computer is not accessible.

To access any shared network folder or device double click on the icon.

The default view of My Network Places lists all shared resources alphabetically by name. You can also arrange the shared resources by computer or network location.

3 Right click anywhere on the white space of the My Network Places window. A drop down menu will appear that gives you several options for arranging the shared resource icons.

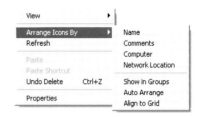

4 Identifying shared resources by their host computer is a useful option. Click Show in Groups and Arrange Icons by Computer to get this display.

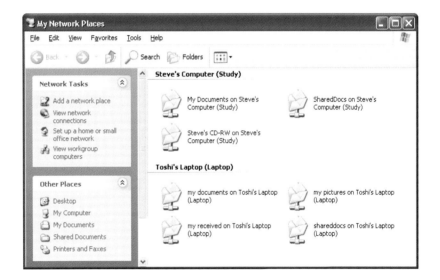

The next chapter will take us out on the road, looking at wireless networking at Wi-Fi hotspots.

If your first goal with wireless is to link up two or more computers in an ad hoc network then jump on to chapter 5, or if you're ready to setup an access point for an infrastructure mode wireless network then turn to chapter 7.

Network Protocols and Services

Protocols and services are software components that your hardware needs to enable communication across your network connections. Windows XP will automatically install the protocols and services needed by your networking hardware. If any of these get accidentally deleted follow these steps to reinstate them.

1 Click Start, Control Panel, Network Connections and right click on the Network Connection you need to update.

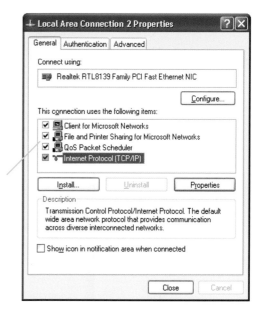

2 The set of protocols and services used by the connection are listed on the General tab as shown here.

If any of these items is missing the connection will not operate correctly.

3 Your network connection, whether wired Ethernet or wireless, should have these four items listed: Client for Microsoft Networks, File and Printer Sharing for Microsoft Networks, QoS Packet Scheduler and Internet Protocol (TCP/IP).

4 If any of these items is missing click Install.

5 Select Client, Service or Protocol and click Add.

Select Service for the File and Printer Sharing or QoS items and Protocol for the Internet Protocol item.

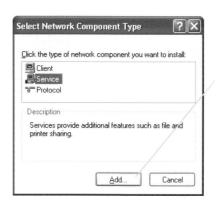

6 Select the item you wish to reinstall from the list of options provided.

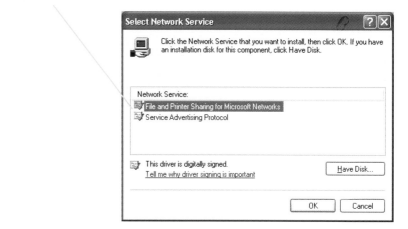

7 Click OK and the required Client, Service or Protocol will be installed.

8 Depending on the item you are installing, you may be prompted to restart Windows XP before the change can become effective.

Internet Protocol (IP) Addressing

Until the advent of Windows XP, setting up the IP addresses of computers on the network was probably the most complex step in building a home network.

In IPv4, the current version of Internet Protocol, addresses are 32-bit binary numbers which are grouped into four 8-bit octets and represented as their decimal equivalents.

IP addresses are the heart of networking; it's these sequences of numbers that enable your computer to find a website on the other side of the world.

Windows XP handles IP address setup automatically for small networks, whether wired or wireless, but it's worthwhile knowing the basic steps in case things don't quite work as planned!

1. Open Network Connections (Click Start, Control Panel, Network Connections or from your desktop shortcut).

2. Right click on the Network Connection you need to update, (Local Area Connection or Wireless Network Connection) and choose Properties from the short menu.

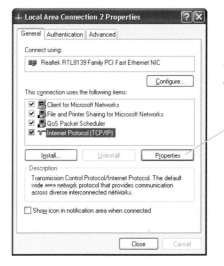

3. On the General tab select Internet Protocol (TCP/IP) and click Properties.

...cont'd

This default uses a Windows XP service named Automatic Private IP Address or APIPA.

4 In the Internet Protocol Properties dialog box the default is Obtain an IP address automatically. Don't change this setting unless you're given specific addresses by a Network Administrator.

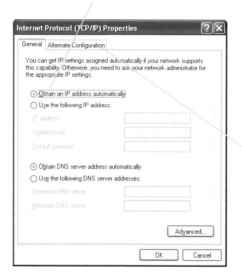

The Alternative Configuration tab is only available if automatic addressing is selected on the General tab.

5 Select the Alternative Configuration tab.

6 If you have more than one network connection on this computer, this tab allows you to set an IP address for a connection where automatic address allocation is not available.

Select Automatic private IP address (APIPA) if you are not connecting to two networks.

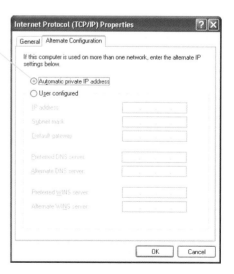

IP addresses run from 0.0.0.0 through to 255.255.255.255. Some ranges are reserved as private IP addresses to be used only in internal networks and not for communication through a router out into the Internet. In fact routers on the Internet will not forward data packets with source or destination addresses in these private ranges.

The reserved ranges for private IP addresses are;

- 10.0.0.0 through 10.255.255.255

- 172.16.0.0 through 172.31.255.255

- 192.168.0.0 through 192.168.255.255

If you need to specify private addresses for one of your network connections, choose one of these ranges and assign sequential addresses to each computer in that segment of the network.

Computers with private IP addresses can still access the Internet using a process called Network Address Translation (NAT) provided by the router connecting your network to the Internet.

This may be needed for example if you have a wireless network with IP addresses automatically assigned by a DHCP server in the access point, and one of your computers also has a simple wired Ethernet connection to another computer with no hub or switch.

7 Select User configured.

8 Enter the IP address for the first computer in this private segment of your network. Click OK.

9 Repeat these steps for the other computer or computers on the segment of your network that requires private addressing. Use sequential numbering for each computer, e.g. the next in this sequence will be 10.0.0.2. The Subnet mask will be unchanged and will be filled in automatically by Windows XP.

Going Mobile: Hotspot Networking

As a first step in wireless networking, this chapter takes you through the steps to connect to the Internet through a Wi-Fi hotspot. Wireless enabling a laptop computer is covered first, then how to find and connect to a hotspot.

Some of the main hotspot services in USA, UK and internationally are introduced, and you'll learn about aspects of security that you should be aware of when using hotspots. Finally we'll take a look at some free non-Windows software for managing hotspot connections.

Covers

Chapter Four

Introducing Wireless Hotspots

Wi-Fi hotspots are public access points to the Internet where the connection between a mobile computer and the Internet is made using a wireless connection.

Some estimates put the number of hotspots in USA at 500,000 by 2007, from only 4,000 at the end of 2002.

Driven both by the large international telecoms operators, as well as small local enterprises, hotspots are springing up by the tens of thousands worldwide. In partnership with venue owners, the early focus is on hotels, airports and coffee shops, with names like Starbucks, Hilton and Borders at the front of the pack.

Hotspots enable you to connect to the Internet or, often using a secure VPN connection, to your corporate network when you're out and about town.

Getting started

To get started using wireless hotspots you need a portable computer, a laptop, notebook or even a PDA, equipped with a wireless network adapter card.

Then you need to find a hotspot location. The service provider's websites that we'll look at later in this chapter provide directories of their own sites, and there are a number of independent directories that give global coverage.

Some of the limitations

Some pay-as-you-go services only let you connect to the hotspot at which you first sign-up!

The hotspot industry is still in its infancy and one of the things that has yet to develop is a comprehensive cross-charging system to allow users to roam between hotspot operators.

The technology to allow roaming between Wi-Fi hotspots is also "work in progress" following the recently ratified IEEE 802.11f standard.

At the moment if you buy access with one operator you can usually only use that operator's hotspots. However, consumer demand is driving progress in this area, and with companies such as iPass and Boingo focusing on aggregation it looks like true global roaming across Wi-Fi hotspots may be on the horizon.

Security is also an issue you need to be aware of when using hotspots. We'll cover this in detail later in this chapter and also in chapter 8.

Wireless Network Adapters for Laptop Computers

The standard wireless network adapter for a laptop computer is an internal adapter card which slots into a free PC slot on the side of your PC. The Linksys WPC11 shown here is a typical example.

If your PC slots are all occupied you can also use a USB wireless adapter for your laptop. See page 71.

Some adapters have an output power of 200mW or more. This is within FCC limits for USA, but in UK a 100mW limit applies for unlicensed wireless devices, less if an external high gain antenna is used (see chapter 9).

This type of adapter has an internal radio antenna. If you think you might want to extend the range of your wireless connection consider buying an adapter with a connector to attach an external antenna. An example is the Buffalo Airstation adapter. Connecting this adapter to an external antenna is covered in chapter 9.

Extending the range of your wireless connection is covered in chapter 9.

Connector to attach external antenna

Look out for the Wi-Fi Alliance's mark on your Wi-Fi gear to ensure interoperability with other manufacturers.

Having chosen your wireless network adapter the next step is to install and configure it for use in your laptop computer.

Installing a Laptop Wireless Network Adapter

In chapter 5 we will install a wireless network adapter into a desktop computer running Windows XP. If your laptop computer is also running Windows XP then follow the installation instructions in chapter 5 for that computer as well. The following steps apply if your laptop is running Windows 98/2000/ME.

If your laptop is running Windows XP do not install the software drivers before installing the hardware.

Installing the wireless adapter in Windows 98/2000/ME

I   Before installing your laptop wireless network adapter card, switch on your laptop and insert the adapter manufacturer's setup CD into your CD-ROM drive.

If your laptop is running a pre-XP Windows version (98/2000/ME) and you plug the adapter in before installing the software the New Hardware Wizard will install the device drivers but won't install the manufacturer's configuration utility.

2   Click Start, Run and navigate to the setup utility on the installation CD. The file will be named Setup.exe or similar. Click OK.

3   The manufacturer's setup utility will start. The details of the setup utility will depend on the manufacturer of the adapter you are installing, but the basic steps will be the same.

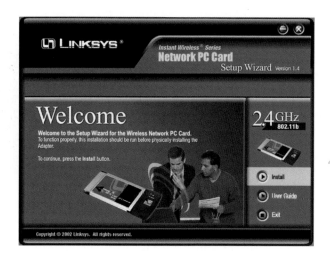

4   Click Install to start the process.

5 Your connection to a hotspot will be in Infrastructure Mode. Check this radio button.

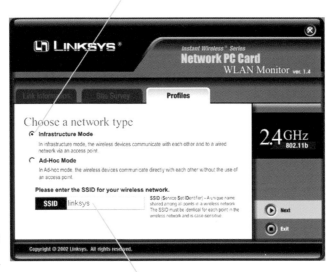

It is generally recommended to change the default SSID to improve the security of your network connection. It doesn't matter in this case as you are going to enter the SSID of the hotspot later.

6 If you know the SSID of the hotspot you are going to connect to enter it here. If not this can be updated when you connect.

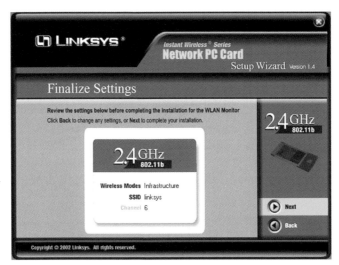

The channel number is grayed out here because in Infrastructure Mode the adapter will sense the channel being used by the hotspot access point.

7 Confirm the settings if required.

You can insert the network adapter without powering down but it is not recommended. Some go as far as disconnecting the power lead before inserting new hardware, but this is probably unnecessarily cautious.

8 Power down the laptop and insert the wireless adapter card.

9 Restart your laptop. Windows will detect the new hardware and install the software drivers.

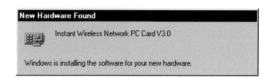

Windows may notify you of a version conflict if the installation process tries to overwrite a file with an older version. It is recommended to keep the newest version.

10 To complete the installation you will be asked to restart your computer.

AP is short for access point, and refers to the device used in hotspots and other Infrastructure mode wireless networks that your network adapter communicates with. See more in chapter 7.

The installation of hardware and software to enable your laptop to make a wireless connection to a hotspot is now completed. Unless you are already sitting within range of the hotspot your network adapter's monitor software will show that you are not yet connected. The next section tells you how to find a hotspot near you, then you'll learn how to make the connection.

Finding a Wireless Hotspot

Wireless Hotspots are being established by a number of telecoms and other operators in a wide range of locations all around the world. The initial emphasis is on business travellers, with hotspots located in airport lounges, hotels and at major railway stations.

The more casual user is catered for by the partnerships springing up between telecom operators and venues such as coffee shops and pubs.

A good place to look for hotspot locations is at the wifinder website www.wifinder.com.

In Canada and USA, some pay phone operators including Bell and Verizon are starting to Wi-Fi enable pay phone kiosks.

Another way to find hotspots is to look out for warchalking symbols, a craze that started in London in 2002. See www.warchalking.org.

Several other hotspot directories are listed in chapter 12, and you can also check out the websites of the main hotspot providers operating in the UK:

- T-Mobile   www.t-mobile.com

- Surf and Sip   www.surfandsip.com

- Swisscom Eurospot www.swisscom.com

- Boingo   www.boingo.com

- BT Openzone   www.bt.com/openzone

Connecting to Hotspot Services

Some operators are starting to bundle hotspot Internet access in with phone or home broadband charging. Look out for an offer from your phone or broadband operator!

Hotspot providers offer a variety of subscription options, ranging from short term access for perhaps a couple of hours up to monthly or annual subscriptions. For your first experiments with hotspot connections you'll probably want to sign up for short term access.

The initial steps to connect to a hotspot are the same for all operators and are covered below. In the following sections you'll see the sign-up procedure of some of the major hotspot operators in more detail.

Initial steps to connect to a hotspot

Don't leave your laptop unattended when you go to get a newspaper or some extra sugar! It might not be there when you get back.

1 Find yourself a comfortable seat in the coffee shop, hotel lobby or airport lounge and switch on your laptop. Right click the Wireless Zero Configuration icon in the notification area.

Click View Available Wireless Networks.

If the Network key input field is grayed out it indicates that the hotspot is not using WEP encryption. See page 60 for more on hotspot security.

2 Select the hotspot service that you wish to connect to from the list of available networks and click Connect.

This establishes the wireless connection.

If you are using a browser other than Internet Explorer and have trouble reaching the login page, try again using IE.

3 Start up your Internet browser. Your browser's Home Page request will be redirected to the welcome page of the hotspot service provider.

4 Follow the steps in the following sections, or on the welcome page for the particular hotspot that you're connecting to.

Hotspots in USA and Canada

There are over a hundred hotspot operators in the USA and this number is likely to grow in the near future, although some shake-out and consolidation seems likely longer term. We'll take a quick look at a few of the major operators.

T-Mobile hotspots

A division of Deutsche Telecom, T-Mobile is becoming a major player both in USA and in Europe, although service offerings vary by region.

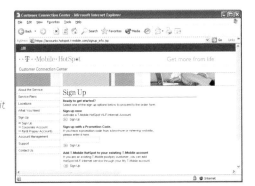

Follow the Sign Up link for information on various service options.

In USA, T-Mobile offers integrated billing and a special unlimited Wi-Fi access rate to existing phone customers.

Take care when entering your credit card or other confidential data in a public place. Make sure no one is looking over your shoulder!

Create a new account online, sign-up using a promotional offer or add Wi-Fi to your existing account if you are already a T-Mobile customer.

With 5,300 locations across USA at airports, and in partnership with Starbucks and Borders, T-Mobile operates two-thirds of all USA hotspots.

AT&T Wireless hotspots

AT&T's GoPort hotspots are available at a large number of airports, hotels and resorts in 50 major cities across USA.

AT&T plans to offer a VPN service for secure links to corporate networks.

The AT&T wireless site at www.attws.com gives full information on connecting, service plans, etc.

You can buy AT&T's Connect service online in advance or at any GoPort location.

The step-by-step sign-up procedure depends on your location.

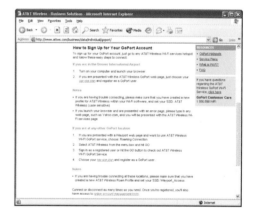

AT&T, IBM and Intel have jointly set up Cometa Networks with a plan to install 10,000 hotspots in coffee shops, hotels, university campuses and other sites across USA.

Check the GoPort Hotspots link to get the latest information on available locations by region.

Verizon Wireless hotspots

Currently providing free hotspot access at locations in New York to existing Verizon customers. If the trial in NY is successful, Verizon plans to extend its Wi-Fi coverage to its other major East Coast markets.

Follow the Getting Connected link for information on connecting to a Verizon hotspot.

Click Locations for up-to-date information on the available hotspot locations in New York.

For information on other hotspots in New York take a look at:

- http://www.downtownny.com, and
- http://publicinternetproject.org

Wayport hotspots

Wayport is a leading hotspot provider in the USA and is pioneering roaming alliances, for example with AT&T, iPass, Boingo and GRIC. This may help pave the way for cross charging arrangements that will allow hotspot users to roam between service providers and not be tied to a single hotspot operator or location.

Wayport started life in the late 1990s as a start-up bringing wired Internet access to business travellers in hotels.

Find information on service plans and pricing from the Wayport Home Page.

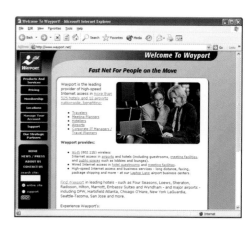

FatPort, Canada

FatPort is Canada's largest public Wi-Fi operator, with locations across the country.

FatPort has a roaming agreement with Airpath (US), Kubi Wireless (Spain), NetWireless (Canada), Oasis Wireless (Canada) and SwissCom (International).

Other hotspot operators in Canada include Oasis Wireless (www.oasiswireless.net) and NetWireless (www.netwireless.ca).

Hotspots in UK and Europe

Hotspots are being rapidly established in the UK and across Europe by a number of operators in partnership with venue owners. Check out www.wifinder.com for the latest on locations.

T-Mobile hotspots

In Europe, T-Mobile is setting up hotspots in partnership with Starbucks.

Buy yourself a nice Grande Latte, Double Espresso, or whatever your favorite beverage, find a comfortable seat and follow the steps on page 50. This will bring up the T-Mobile home page.

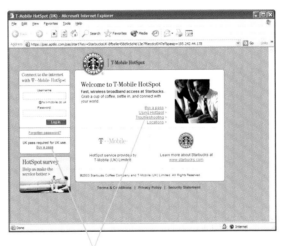

Click Buy a Pass either from the central menu or from the login panel on the left and follow the sign-up procedure.

Make a note of the Username and Password in case there is an interruption in your connection before you can access the confirmation email.

When you have completed the sign-up you can use the links on the Your Session dialog to find other T-Mobile locations or to troubleshoot your connection.

Surf and Sip hotspots

Operating in Europe in partnership with Internet Exchange Internet cafes.

1   Find yourself a comfortable seat and follow the initial steps described on page 50. This will bring up the Surf and Sip welcome page.

2   If you have purchased a prepaid access card enter the card number as it appears on the back of the card. Otherwise, click Sign Up! and you'll be asked to select the service plan you want to sign up for.

Make a note of the Username and Password as the Surf and Sip email confirmation does not remind you what you entered!

3   Once you have created an account and entered your payment details click Login and this will take you back to the welcome page. Enter the Username and Password you chose when creating your account.

4   When you log in successfully your browser will load the surfandsip.com home page. You can now start to surf the Internet.

BT Openzone hotspots

BT Openzone is building a hotspot network in the UK together with Hilton Hotels, UK airports and Costa Coffee.

Don't get too comfortable until Windows XP has connected to the hotspot with at least a good or very good signal strength. If you're in an area with low signal strength you may have to move! Alternatively, if your wireless NIC has an antenna connector, check out the DIY antenna designs in chapter 9.

Complete your check-in, go through to the departure lounge, find a comfortable seat and follow the initial steps described on page 50. When your browser starts up this will take you to the BT Openzone welcome page.

Select Create a new account from the menu on the left.

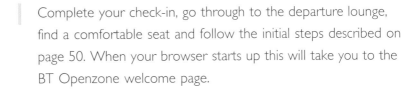

Don't forget to make a note of your Login and Password.

Once you have created an account, login and click the Top Up My Account link to buy your Internet Access pass.

Other European hotspot operators

Elsewhere in Europe, check out:

www.kasteurope.net in France,

www.monzoon.net in Germany and Switzerland,

www.hubhop.com in the Netherlands,

www.aptilo.com in Denmark, and

www.swisscom.com for hotspots throughout Europe.

International Hotspots

The rest of the world is not being left behind in the hotspot stakes, with a wide variety of local enterprises starting hotspots as well as the major international operators.

If you're travelling for business or vacation and want to stay connected take your laptop and wireless adapter along with you.

Australia, Azure Wireless
A 2002 start-up with hotspots in hotels, convention centers, cafes and airports in Melbourne and Sydney, and plans to extend its coverage to Adelaide, Brisbane, Canberra and Perth.

Azure and Boingo have a global roaming agreement.

Hong Kong, Systech Telecom
A Hong Kong start-up that operates hotspots in hotels and shopping centers around the island.

Systech offers free wireless adapter hire at hotel receptions for hotel guests.

Free access is available at some of the shopping mall locations. Prepaid cards can be purchased at hotel receptions.

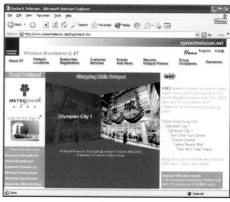

Singapore, StarHub

A local operator with a growing hotspot network currently covering Suntec City and Changi Airport.

StarHub has a global roaming agreement with iPass and GRIC

Malaysia, Maxis

Maxis hotspots, called Utopia WLAN Zones, can be found at a large number of cafes, restaurants, hotels and other venues around Kuala Lumpur and Petaling Jaya.

Maxis also offers VPN and a low cost voice over IP (VoIP) phone service.

Philippines, Airborne Access

A March 2002 start-up that is quickly building a hotspot network in major cities in the Philippines, partnering Netopia Internet Cafes and Seattle's best coffee shops.

The site also offers a helpful guide to setting up the most popular wireless adapters.

Japan has a wide network of free hotspots. See the site listings from www.wifinder.com or www.wififreespot.com for info.

Hotspot Security

Wireless network security is covered further in chapter 8.

To make hotspots easily accessible for public users, the security features such as data encryption that are available for wireless networking are generally disabled.

This means that most communications from your computer such as web based email will be transmitted as clear, unencrypted text and may be vulnerable to illicit interception.

Although it may seem unlikely that hackers would target hotspot users, there are a number of measures you should consider taking in order to ensure that your data and resources are as secure as possible.

Using a Personal Firewall

A variety of personal firewall products are available, including several freeware downloads. As a hotspot user they can protect you from the action of other hotspot users and also make you aware of any malicious applications that may try to access your resources.

Windows XP's Internet Connection Firewall is covered on page 86.

Information on personal firewalls can be found at www.firewall.com...

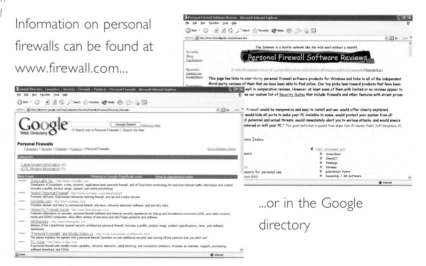

...or in the Google directory

Make sure your personal firewall and antivirus software are enabled and keep them up to date with the latest upgrades.

Using Antivirus Software

Antivirus software will protect your resources from the effects of viruses and other "attack vectors" that may attempt to infect your computer from the network. Perhaps equally important, this type of software could save you the embarrassment of infecting other users that you may connect to.

Apply the latest Windows Service Packs

You can either use Windows XP's automatic update service or else connect directly to the Microsoft support website to download the latest operating system updates and service packs.

Keeping your system up to date will improve its performance as well as security.

Windows XP upgrades and service packs can be accessed from the Microsoft website at http://support.microsoft.com.

Watch out for SSL Security

If you connect to a secure site, your data will be encrypted using secure socket layer (SSL) technology.

SSL is the current standard method for encrypting secure transactions across the Internet.

You can recognize a secure Internet site either by the https:// address in your browser address window,

or by the locked padlock in the notification area in the bottom right of the browser. You will usually see https:// being used when you provide credit card details, or change your password or other confidential data.

Check with your email service provider to see if they offer a secure email service.

Hotspot service providers generally recommend not to use web based email to transmit confidential information and if possible to encrypt any email attachments before sending them.

A hotspot provider's VPN service may secure the wireless connection, but sensitive data could still be vulnerable when routed on from the hotspot provider. Consider encrypting sensitive data unless the VPN connection goes all the way to your data's destination.

VPN Security

Some hotspot operators offer the security of a Virtual Private Network or VPN connection.

Keep sensitive passwords secure

If you have passwords to sensitive information on your computer don't reuse these on hotspots where your user information may be transmitted unencrypted and therefore open to eavesdropping.

Disable your wireless network adapter when not in use

If you are using your laptop in the open but not connected to a hotspot, then it is good practice to disable your wireless adapter.

1   Right click on the Wireless Network Connection icon in your notification area.

2   Click Disable. To re-enable your Wireless Adapter repeat step 1 and click Enable.

Don't auto-connect to non-preferred networks

It is possible for a hacker to setup a bogus access point that looks to your computer like a bona fide hotspot. Depending on your Wireless Zero Configuration settings your computer may automatically associate with the access point, providing a possible entry route to your computer.

1   Open Network Connections, double click your Wireless Network Connection. On the Wireless Networking tab click the Advanced button.

2   Uncheck the Automatically connect to non-preferred networks check box.

3   Click Close and OK.

Using a non-Windows Connection Manager

As an alternative to using Windows XP to manage your hotspot and other wireless connections, you might want to consider third party software which may have useful extra features.

The connection manager available as a free download from Boingo is a typical example, which offers a graphical signal strength monitor as well as some additional auto connection options that may be useful if you expect to connect to several different networks.

Downloading and installing the Boingo software

A PDA version of the Boingo software is also available to allow you to connect and surf using a wireless enabled PDA (see page 160).

Connect to the Internet, start up your browser and enter the Boingo website address into your browser's address window.

When the Boingo home page opens, click Software to begin downloading the Boingo installer.

3 Follow the instructions to download the Boingo installer file to your desktop.

4 Double click the Boingo installer icon to begin installation.

5 Follow the instructions and click Next at each step.

6 Enter your name and email address when requested.

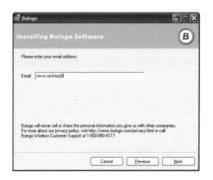

7 When software installation has completed, click the Read the manual? check box if you want to look at the documentation.

8 The Boingo shortcut will appear on your desktop when installation is completed, and a B symbol will appear in the notification area when the Boingo software is running.

Connecting using the Boingo connection manager

When you start-up or restart your laptop computer, Boingo will automatically load and search for available wireless networks. Click the Connect button to connect to an identified network.

WEP, or Wired Equivalent Privacy, is a privacy mechanism based on encryption that is intended to give a wireless network the same level of privacy as a wired network. See chapter 8 for more on WEP and wireless security.

If WEP is enabled on the network, Boingo will ask you for the Network key. Enter the key value and click OK.

Boingo will connect to the selected network, as indicated by the Status button.

Creating and editing profiles in the Boingo connection manager

Profiles allow you to keep the setup parameters for a number of frequently used network connections.

1 Click Profiles and then select My Signal Profiles.

2 Select the profile you want to edit or click Add to create a new profile.

For hotspot connections you will need to specify Infrastructure mode.

Some networks do not broadcast their SSID as an added security measure.

3 The Network tab of the Profile Editor allows you to specify a Profile Name, Network SSID and network mode.

In hotspots WEP is usually disabled, but your hotspot operator will tell you if you need to use a WEP key.

4 The WEP Key tab allows you to specify whether WEP is enabled and to enter the WEP key.

The auto-run feature would allow you to run an email program or VPN (Virtual Private Network) security software if you are connecting to a corporate network. See chapter 8 for more on network security.

5 The Autoconnect tab allows you to specify your preferences for which network to connect to if several are available. You can also specify a program to run automatically when a particular network is connected to.

The IP address uniquely identifies your computer on the Internet. DHCP is a service which automatically gives your computer an IP address when you connect to the network.

6 The IP Settings tab is for advanced users only. Use the DHCP option unless you are told otherwise by a network administrator.

Using other Boingo features

Under **Find a Location** you can access a directory and details of Boingo hotspots, searchable by country and city.

Click Details and then **Signal Performance** and you will find a graphical signal strength monitor. This can be useful to optimize your location if you are finding it difficult to get good reception.

If Boingo attempts to connect to the Internet to get the latest updates and fails to make a connection it may continuously open new browser windows on your screen. Right click the B icon in the notification area and choose Exit Boingo. You will then be able to close down the unwanted windows.

Under Profiles and then **Preferences** you will be able to enable or disable automatic software and directory updates.

Ad hoc Wireless Networking

This chapter shows you how to setup an ad hoc or peer-to-peer wireless network in order to share files, printers or other resources between two or more computers.

You will learn about the different types of wireless network adapters available for desktop computers, install and configure a network adapter, and setup an ad hoc connection using Windows XP. Finally you'll see how to maintain security using Wired Equivalent Privacy (WEP).

Covers

Chapter Five

Introduction

Having successfully installed a wireless adapter and connected to a hotspot, the next step in wireless networking is to connect two or more computers together in a simple network to share files or other resources.

The other type of connection, called infrastructure mode, is covered in chapter 7.

This type of connection is known as an ad hoc or peer-to-peer network, and is one of the two varieties of wireless link that are defined in the Wi-Fi or 802.11 wireless network standards.

Windows XP includes a service called Zero Configuration which enables automatic switching between network modes. Check your chosen adapter for Windows XP compatibility to ensure this feature is available.

An ad hoc network connecting several computers, which could be desktops, laptops, PDAs or, in the near future, other network ready home electronic devices or domestic appliances.

Each of the computers in an ad hoc network communicates equally with all other computers in the network, without any central hub or access point to direct network traffic.

As we saw in the introduction on page 10, network communication is a multilevel process, and the setup requires hardware and software to be installed to make the links at several levels of the OSI model.

Firstly, two or more computers each with wireless network adapters installed and correctly configured complete the physical link. Secondly, ensuring that the software components are in place and configured on all computers to allow them to establish network communications, and finally enabling shared access to files and other resources.

We looked at enabling shared access to network resources in chapter 2, after setting up a wired network. In this chapter we'll cover installing and configuring the hardware and software.

Wireless Network Adapters for Desktop Computers

In chapter 4 we looked at wireless network adapters for laptops. If your ad hoc network is going to connect a laptop to your desktop computer, the desktop also needs to have a wireless adapter fitted. There are two basic types of wireless adapters available for desktop computers – internal and external.

An internal adapter card requires a spare PCI slot inside your desktop PC, and the Linksys WMP11 is a typical example.

Internal adapters have the advantage that the antenna is often attached to the card using a removable connection, which allows an external antenna to be connected. This can be useful if you want to extend the range of your network.

Extending the range of your network is covered in chapter 9.

Internal adapters are also available that allow you to install a laptop PC wireless adapter card into a desktop PCI slot.

An external adapter, such as the Linksys WUSB11, will attach to your computer through a USB port. USB devices can be "daisy chained", which means that you can plug the wireless network adapter into any spare USB port, for example on your monitor, not just into a USB port directly on your desktop computer.

Installing a Wireless Adapter in Windows XP

In chapter 4 we installed a wireless network adapter into a computer running pre-XP Windows 98/2000/ME.

If your second computer is also running an older version of Windows, follow the same steps for that computer. The following steps will apply if your second computer is running Windows XP.

Installing the wireless adapter in Windows XP

Do not install the software drivers before installing the hardware if your computer is running Windows XP. You should only install drivers first for computers running older versions of Windows such as 98/2000/ME.

1 Switch off your computer and install the wireless adapter, either by inserting into a spare PCI slot, or by plugging into a spare USB port, depending on the type of adapter you have purchased.

2 Switch on your computer and Windows XP will automatically detect the new hardware and start the New Hardware Wizard.

3 Select Install from a specific location and click Next.

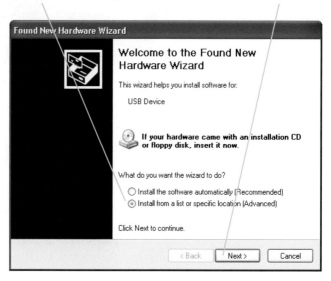

4 Select Search for the best drivers in these locations and Include this location in the search.

Use the Browse button to navigate your way to the installation CD.

5 Indicate the location of the device drivers on your installation CD and click Next.

Follow the steps under Network Setup Using Windows XP on page 24.

6 Click Finish. Your hardware is now installed. The next step is to setup a network connection, as described in chapter 3.

Connecting to an Ad hoc Wireless Network

Windows XP Zero Configuration will switch the wireless network adapter between ad hoc & infrastructure modes depending on the selected network.

After installing the network adapter hardware and software driver, the Windows XP Zero Configuration icon will appear in the notification area. To connect to an existing ad hoc network follow these steps. If you need to setup a new ad hoc connection in Windows XP skip forward to the next section.

Some older network adapters may not support Windows XP Zero Configuration.

1   Start up one or more of the other computers in the ad hoc network and ensure that their wireless cards are installed and operating correctly.

2   Right click on the Wireless XP Zero Configuration icon and select View Available Wireless Networks

3   If more than one available network is shown, select the SSID of the network you wish to connect to.

To be active, WEP has to be enabled with the same key on all computers that are to be connected together in the network.

If WEP has not been enabled on the other computers the Network key input field will be grayed out and inactive.

4   If WEP is enabled on the other computers in the network enter the Network key and click Connect.

If you've already made a wireless network connection and WEP is then changed from disabled to enabled on the other computers in the network, the properties for this connection will need to be manually reconfigured. This is described on page 78.

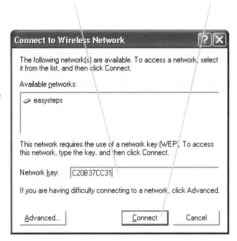

5   The Wireless Network Connection bubble will appear in the notification area once the connection is made.

6   You can check the status of your wireless connection at any time by clicking on the Windows XP Zero Connection icon.

Wireless Network Connection status only shows the status of the physical link and does not show whether resources are accessible across the link. For example if WEP is not correctly configured the status will still show as connected although you will not be able to reach shared resources. See Network Troubleshooting, chapter 10.

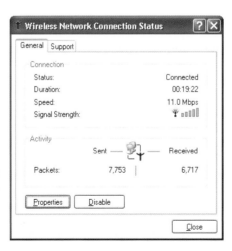

Creating a New Ad hoc Wireless Network

The last section showed you how to connect to an ad hoc network that had been set up on another computer. In this section you will learn how to set up a new ad hoc wireless network connection using Windows XP.

1 Click Start, Settings, Network Connections and double click Wireless Network Connection.

2 In the Wireless Network Connection dialog box click Properties

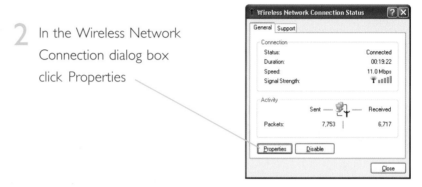

3 In the Wireless Network Connection Properties dialog box select the Wireless Networks tab and click Advanced.

4 Select Computer-to-computer (ad hoc) networks only.

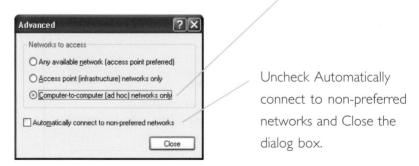

Uncheck Automatically connect to non-preferred networks and Close the dialog box.

5 Under Preferred networks on the Wireless Network Connection Properties dialog box click Add.

6 In the Wireless network properties dialog box enter an SSID name for your new ad hoc network.

The format of this dialog box will be different if you have upgraded Windows XP with the SP1/WPA updates (see page 116).

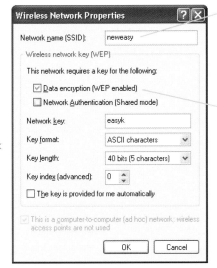

7 Select Data encryption and enter a Network key if you want to enable WEP.

The ASCII Network key entry will only work with other Windows XP clients. If using hardware manufacturer's client software on other computers you will have to reenter the hexadecimal Network key when connecting.

8 Click OK and your new network connection will appear in the Preferred networks list. The red x on the icon indicates that no other computers are connected to the network.

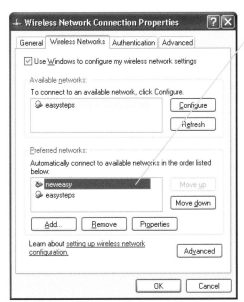

If you are using WEP you will have to let other users know the Network key in order for them to connect.

Other wireless enabled computers within range will now be able to see your ad hoc network and connect to it.

Maintaining Security for Ad hoc Networks

Even for an ad hoc network the transmitted wireless signal can propagate over distances of several hundred meters, depending on the type of location. For maximum security you should ensure that:

If WEP is enabled on one computer but not on the other you will not be able to access shared files or other resources.

- WEP (Wired Equivalent Privacy) is enabled on all computers in the ad hoc network.

- Each network adapter is correctly configured using the same WEP key.

If WEP is switched from disabled to enabled on a computer in an ad hoc network, the properties of the wireless network connection on the other computers will need to be updated in order to connect correctly.

Changing WEP status for an existing connection

1   Right click the Windows XP Zero Configuration icon and click View Available Wireless Connections.

2   In the Connect to Wireless Network dialog box the Network key input field is inactive, although WEP has been enabled on the other computers. Click Advanced.

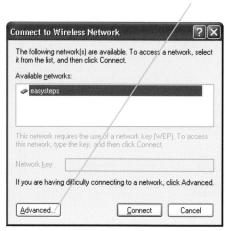

3 Select the connection you want to update from the Preferred networks list and click Properties.

To change properties make sure you select from the Preferred networks list rather than the Available networks list.

4 Click Data encryption and then click to uncheck The key is provided for me automatically.

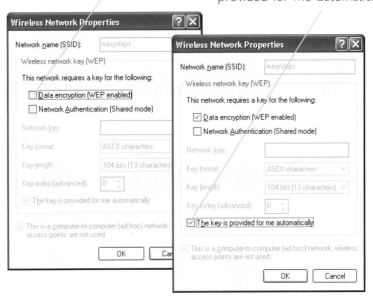

5 Enter the Network key into the input field and click OK.

The Network key can be a 5 or 13 character ASCII string, or a 10 or 26 digit string of hexadecimal characters.

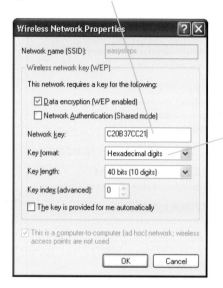

Wireless Network Properties

Network name (SSID): easysteps

Wireless network key (WEP)

This network requires a key for the following:

☑ Data encryption (WEP enabled)
☐ Network Authentication (Shared mode)

Network key: C20B37CC21|

Key format: Hexadecimal digits

Key length: 40 bits (10 digits)

Key index (advanced): 0

☐ The key is provided for me automatically

☑ This is a computer-to-computer (ad hoc) network; wireless access points are not used

OK   Cancel

The Key format and Key length will be automatically selected based on the format of the Network key you have entered.

Some wireless hardware uses a set of four keys, from which one is selected using the Key index. Only change this value if you have setup other network hardware using a nonzero value for the key index.

6 Click OK again in the Wireless Network Properties dialog box. The Connect to Wireless Network dialog box will reappear with the Network key input field active, indicating that WEP is now enabled for this connection.

Connect to Wireless Network

The following network(s) are available. To access a network, select it from the list, and then click Connect.

Available networks:

📶 easysteps

This network requires the use of a network key (WEP). To access this network, type the key, and then click Connect.

Network key:

If you are having difficulty connecting to a network, click Advanced.

Advanced...   Connect   Cancel

Windows XP can be reluctant to let go of the old settings if you try to enable WEP on an active ad hoc network. Switch off the other computers and enable WEP one computer at a time.

7 Windows XP will now re-establish a connection to the available network with WEP enabled, using the Network key you entered.

Advanced Networking Options

Following on from chapter 3, where we looked at basic networking under Windows XP, in this chapter you'll learn some more advanced networking options.

First we look at sharing an Internet connection using Windows XP, and at managing the Internet connection from a remote computer. We'll learn about the Windows Internet Connection Firewall and finish with a run through some network performance monitoring tools.

Covers

Chapter Six

Internet Connection Sharing (ICS)

As we saw in chapter 3 when setting up the network, Internet Connection Sharing in Windows XP allows you to configure one computer in your network as a host through which all other workgroup computers can connect to the Internet.

Changing ICS Host Settings

The host computer must be switched on for other computers to be able to use its Internet connection.

1 To access ICS settings, open Network Connections from your Desktop or from the Start menu on the computer that hosts your Internet connection and right click the shared Internet Connection icon.

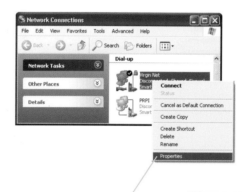

2 Choose Properties and in the Properties dialog box click Advanced.

The Internet Connection Firewall is also enabled on the Advanced tab. ICF is covered later in this chapter.

3 Check or clear the Allow other network users to connect through this computer's Internet connection to enable or disable ICS.

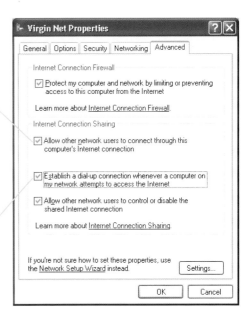

If the check box is cleared other computers will only be able to access the Internet when the host computer has opened the connection.

4 Check the Establish a dial-up connection... check box if you want Windows XP to automatically make the connection when a workgroup computer tries to access the Internet. This option only appears if you are sharing a dial-up connection.

Checking this box enables Windows XP's ICS Discovery and Control service.

5 If you check the box to Allow other network users to control or disable the shared Internet connection, each workgroup computer will be able to control the shared connection as if it was the host. ICS connection management is covered next.

Managing a Shared Internet Connection

If you have allowed other network users to control or disable the shared Internet connection, then even if these users do not have direct access to the host computer they will still be able to view connection statistics, monitor the status of the connection and connect to or disconnect from your ISP.

Connecting to the Internet using ICS

1 Open Network Connections from your Desktop or from the Start menu. If network computers' control of the dial-up connection is enabled you will see a group called Internet Gateway in the folder.

2 Right click the icon for your Internet connection and select Connect from the drop down menu.

3 Windows XP will open the shared Internet connection and let you know that it is trying to connect.

4 When the connection is made a bubble will appear above the notification area.

5 In the Network Connections folder the Internet Gateway will now be shown as Connected.

Viewing Internet connection status

Right click on the icon for the shared Internet connection in the notification area and select Status.

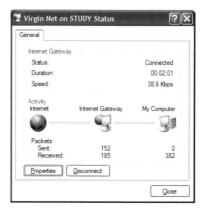

You will be able to check your connection speed and how many data packets have been sent and received through the gateway to the Internet.

Disconnecting a shared Internet connection

Right click on the icon for the shared Internet connection in Network Connections and select Disconnect, or click Disconnect in the Status dialog box above.

In Network Connections the Internet Gateway will now be shown as Disconnected.

Using Internet Connection Firewall

ICF should not be used if you are using a residential gateway or access point to connect to the Internet. Use the firewall product that comes with your gateway.

Once you have established a connection to the Internet from your network you should consider using the Windows XP Internet Connection Firewall (ICF) to prevent unwanted access to your computer from the Internet.

ICF works by keeping track of the IP addresses of Internet sites that you are connecting to and only accepting incoming data packets that originated from a recognized IP address.

Enabling the Internet Connection Firewall

1 Open Network Connections from your Desktop or click Start, Connect To, Show all connections.

If your network has more than one Internet connection you need to enable ICF on each connection.

2 Right click on the Internet connection you want to protect and select Properties.

3 Select the Advanced tab.

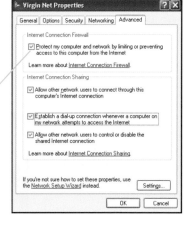

Only enable ICF on connections to the Internet. If you enable ICF on other network computers you will interrupt traffic on your network.

4 On the Advanced tab, check the Protect my computer and network... check box. ICF is now activated.

Enabling the ICF Log File

ICF does not protect your network from attack by viruses or Trojan horse programs that enter via email attachments. Use antivirus software to protect against this type of attack.

When ICF is activated, you can configure the firewall to keep a record of events such as dropped packets or successful connections. You can then view the log file to see what activity has taken place across the firewall.

1   Open Network Connections and right click on the Internet connection. Select Properties.

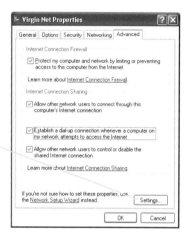

2   Select the Advanced tab in the Properties dialog box, and click the Settings button.

The Settings button is only active if ICF is enabled (step 4 in the previous topic).

3   On the Security Logging tab, select the events that you want to log; Log dropped packets, Log successful connections or both.

You can change the size limit of the log up to 32MB. When the file reaches its maximum size the contents are written to a new file called pfirewall.log. I and new data is collected in pfirewall.log. You will occasionally need to do some housekeeping and delete old files!

4   Change the log file name or location if you want to store it somewhere other than in the default location, and click OK.

Viewing the ICF Log File

When ICF is activated, you can view the log file by opening it with a text editor such as Notepad. The log file contains information about dropped packets or successful connections in time order.

1 Open Notepad by clicking Start, All Programs, Accessories, Notepad.

If you chose a filename or directory other than the default, look there for the log file.

2 Open the log file in Notepad by clicking File, Open, My Computer, Local Drive (C:), WINDOWS, pfirewall.log.

After the header information, each line in the log file records an action on an incoming or outgoing data packet. The first 6 fields record:

Date, Time

Action – such as opening or closing a connection or dropping a packet

Protocol – mostly TCP

Source IP address – the address of the computer that initiated the communication

Destination IP address – the address of the computer that received the communication.

Using the ICF Log File to Monitor Internet Traffic

The information saved in the ICF log file can be used to monitor which websites have been accessed over the ICF protected Internet connection. Each log entry where the action is Open, is a request from a user to open a connection to the website indicated by the destination address. To identify the website follow these steps:

1. Open the log file in Notepad by clicking File, Open, My Computer, Local Drive (C:), WINDOWS, pfirewall.log.

2. For the Open connection that you want to trace, double click the destination IP address (the second of the two IP addresses on the line), then right click and select Copy.

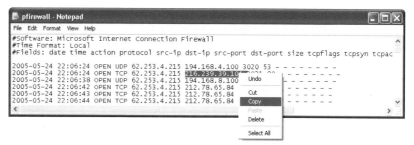

3. Paste the address into the Address field in your browser and click Go. The browser will open a connection to the IP address and the web page will appear.

Monitoring Network Performance

Windows XP provides a set of tools to allow you to monitor the throughput and speed performance of your network. You may want to use these tools if you find that data transfer between parts of your network is slow and you want to look for any bottlenecks.

Network performance using Windows Task Manager

You can also start Task Manager by pressing Ctrl + Alt + Del.

1 Start Windows Task Manager by right clicking in the Task Bar and selecting Task Manager.

2 Select the Networking tab on the Windows Task Manager dialog box.

If you only have one active network connection then the tab will only display one graph.

3 The Networking tab shows you real time information about the utilization of each of the active network adapters on your computer.

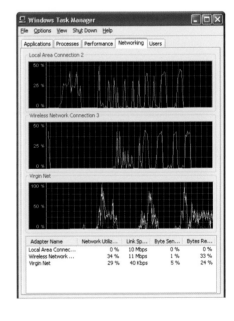

Running Windows Task Manager on the computer that hosts a shared Internet connection can be useful to see if large files are being downloaded elsewhere in the network that may affect performance.

4 You can change the update speed of the graph by clicking View, Update Speed, or you can select to view bytes sent and received as well as total traffic by clicking View, Network Adapter History and selecting the information you want to graph.

5 The data displayed below the network performance graphs can also be customized by clicking View, Select Columns...

6 Select the data items that you wish to monitor from the list.

Managing Performance

Windows XP includes an advanced performance management tool called Performance.

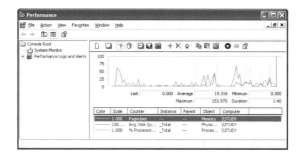

To start Performance click Start, Control panel, Administrative Tools, Performance.

2 To select the items you want to monitor, ensure System Monitor is selected in the left-hand pane and click the New Counter Set button. Click the Add button.

Roll your mouse over the other toolbar buttons to check out some additional features of the Performance tool.

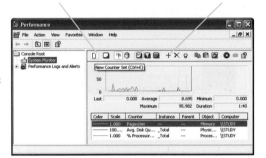

3 In the Add Counters dialog box, select Network Interface from the drop down list of Performance objects.

4 Select the network adapter you want to monitor from the list of instances.

5 Select the data you want to monitor and click the Add button to include each item in the performance chart. Click Close to complete your selection.

You can also use Performance to create a log file of data for later viewing, or to send a notification when a performance measure moves outside a preset range.

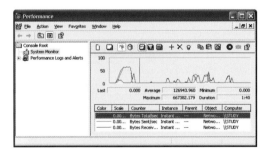

6 The chart will display the performance items you have selected.

Infrastructure Mode Wireless Networking

In this chapter you'll learn about wireless networking in infrastructure mode, where a central access point is used as a hub for wireless communication and as a gateway to the Internet.

We'll look at choosing an access point for a home or small office network, installing and configuring the access point and setting up advanced configuration options.

Covers

Chapter Seven

Introduction to Infrastructure Mode

As we noted in chapter 5, the IEEE 802.11 wireless networking standard supports two types of wireless connections between computers, ad hoc or peer-to-peer mode in which computers in the network communicate directly with each other, and infrastructure mode in which all communication is via a central access point.

The access point (AP) provides a link or bridge between a wired and a wireless network. In a small or not so small office setting there may be several APs connected to the wired network in order to provide wide area coverage for staff to connect using wireless equipped laptops.

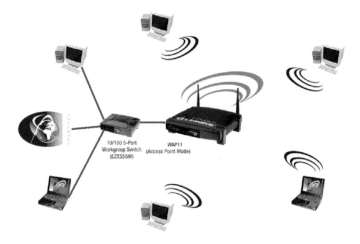

10/100 5-Port
Workgroup Switch
(EZXS55W)

WAP11
(Access Point Mode)

An AP may provide a number of functions in addition to giving wireless access into the wired network, such as;

Most of these functions are also provided by the host computer in an ad hoc wireless network with Windows XP running ICS and ICF. An AP has the advantage that it does not tie up the host computer and provides additional functions when combined with a switch/router.

- Internet connection sharing

- DHCP server for allocating IP addresses

- NAT to keep internal IP addresses private

- Wireless access control and security

- Internet connection security and filtering (firewall)

- Network traffic switching and routing.

Access Points for Home and Small Office Networks

Access points come in a wide range of configurations, from a simple bridge between wired and wireless LANs, to full feature APs combined with switch, router, print server and broadband modem.

A basic AP like the WAP11 will also give you wireless bridging capabilities. See page 130 for wireless bridging.

If your goal is simply to provide a hub for a number of wireless enabled computers to connect to an existing wired network then a simple access point such as the Linksys WAP11 or Buffalo Airstation WLAL11G will do the job.

Some gateways include a printer server feature, allowing printer sharing without a host PC being switched on.

In most cases sharing an Internet connection is a key requirement. Wireless gateways are available from a range of manufacturers. For example, the Linksys WRT54G includes a 4-port Ethernet switch as well as router and 802.11g wireless.

After ratification of the IEEE 802.11g standard in June 2003 a key decision is whether to go for the faster "Wireless G" gear. Check for interoperability certification by the WCA.

Check out sites like 80211planet (see page 166) for info and reviews of all the latest gear.

At the full-feature end of the range, products like the SMC7404 WBRA include all of the above, plus a printer port and a DSL modem to give you a complete broadband and printer sharing solution in one box.

Installing the Router and Configuring Network PCs

The router will manage Internet traffic from your wired and wireless network through to your broadband Internet connection. After wiring the router into your network your PC's configurations will need to be checked to make sure they are setup to work with the router.

Connecting the router to your wired network

1 Power down all your network hardware before you start wiring up.

2 Connect an Ethernet network cable between the Ethernet port on your PC and one of the ports on the back of your router.

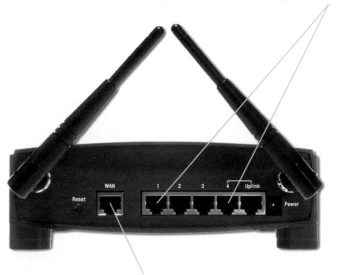

This port may be labeled WAN or Internet, but make sure you connect your modem and router through the correct port.

3 Connect another Ethernet cable between your broadband Internet modem and the WAN or Internet port on the back of the router.

4 Power up your network hardware. The router's front panel LED should light up for the port connected to your PC, indicating that the Ethernet link is active.

Checking PC Configuration

Your PC needs to be configured to obtain an IP address from the router and must also have the TCP/IP protocol installed and available for use. Check this as follows:

If your Control Panel is in Category View, click Switch to Classic View in the task panel.

1 Open Network Connections either from your desktop icon or from Start, Control Panel, Network Connections.

2 Double click the Local Area Network connection and click Properties.

3 On the General tab, verify that the Internet Protocol (TCP/IP) box is checked.

If TCP/IP is not checked, follow the steps on page 38 to install this protocol.

4 Click Internet Protocol and click Properties.

5 On the General tab, verify that the Obtain an IP address automatically radio button is selected.

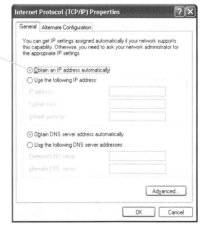

6 Click OK.

If you have not yet run the Network Setup Wizard (page 24) you will need to do so now.

The same settings will need to be checked on the other PCs in the network, including those that will be using wireless links to the access point/router.

Basic Access Point/Router Configuration

To get your access point/router up and running you will need to update some basic settings that configure your Internet access and your wireless mode. More advanced options will be covered in the next section.

Accessing the configuration utility

You should change the default password to ensure security of your network. See under Advanced Options page 101.

1 Your access point/router will probably have a web based configuration utility. Enter its IP address in the address field of your browser.

2 Changing configuration settings will require you to enter an administration password. Check your manufacturer's documentation and enter the required default password.

Some APs have a configuration port, usually a USB port, as an alternative to using a web based utility.

3 The initial setup screen for your configuration utility will be displayed in the browser window.

The specific layout of the setup utility for your hardware may differ from the one shown, but the basic settings you will have to update will be very similar.

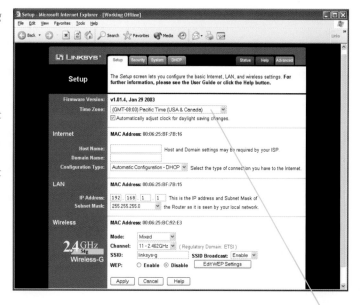

4 The first configuration step is to select your time zone and enable automatic clock changes.

...cont'd

5 If required by your ISP, enter the Host Name and Domain Name.

The MAC address shown here is the address of the port to which your Internet cable is connected.

Internet	MAC Address: 00:06:25:BF:7B:16
Host Name:	Host and Domain settings may be required by your ISP.
Domain Name:	
Configuration Type:	Automatic Configuration - DHCP ▾ Select the type of connection you have to the Internet.

6 Select the Internet configuration type for your Internet connection from the drop down menu.

Configuration Type:	Automatic Configuration - DHCP ▾ Select the type of connection you have to the Internet.
	Automatic Configuration - DHCP
LAN	Static IP
	PPPoE
	PPTP

7 If your ISP connection does not use DHCP, you will be asked to provide additional information.

For **Static IP** you'll need the IP address, Subnet mask, Default Gateway and a Domain Name Server (DNS) IP address.

Configuration Type:	Static IP ▾ Select the type of connection you have to the Internet.
Internet IP Address:	0 . 0 . 0 . 0
Subnet Mask:	0 . 0 . 0 . 0
Gateway:	0 . 0 . 0 . 0
DNS (Required):	1: 0 . 0 . 0 . 0
	2: 0 . 0 . 0 . 0
	3: 0 . 0 . 0 . 0

For **PPPoE** you'll need your User Name and Password.

PPPoE is used sometimes by DSL-based ISPs. The information you need to enter can be obtained from your ISP.

Configuration Type:	PPPoE ▾ Select the type of connection you have to the Internet.
User Name:	
Password:	
○ **Connect on Demand: Max Idle Time**	5 **Min.**
⊙ **Keep Alive: Redial Period**	30 **Sec.**

PPTP is only used in Europe.

For **PPTP** you'll need an IP address, Subnet Mask, Default Gateway, User Name and Password.

8 Lastly, configure the access point's wireless settings. If you have an 802.11g AP, Mixed mode will allow your network to operate with both 802.11g and 802.11b equipped computers.

Don't forget to change the SSID from its default value. This and disabling the SSID broadcast are recommended security practices.

You can select the wireless channel and SSID, just as we saw when setting up an ad hoc wireless network. An additional feature in infrastructure mode is that you can disable the SSID broadcast.

WEP setup is as we saw in chapter 5, with the option of ASCII or Hexadecimal keys, or key generation from a passphrase.

The passphrase option is generally specific to a particular manufacturer. You will need to manually enter the resulting keys if your wireless adapters are from different manufacturers.

Advanced Access Point/Router Configuration

If you haven't done so you will also need to run the Windows Network Setup Wizard (see page 24).

With the basic settings of your access point/router setup as described in the last section, your infrastructure mode wireless network will be up and running, and your networked computers, whether wired or wireless, will be able to connect to your ISP through the router.

Your AP/router will have a range of more advanced functions including security and network management. In this section we take a look at some of these features.

Security

On the Security tab you will be able to set an administration password for the configuration utility. Change the default password to prevent unauthorized access to your network settings.

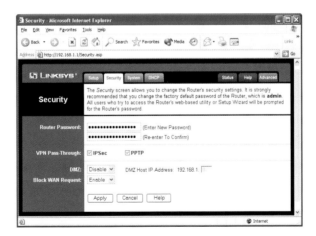

Most routers support VPN passthrough which is used in an office setting to allow secure access from the Internet into the office network.

You may want to enable one PC on your network to operate as a DMZ host if you want to host websites or for Internet games.

General settings

A general settings tab will allow you to control some of the general features of your AP/router.

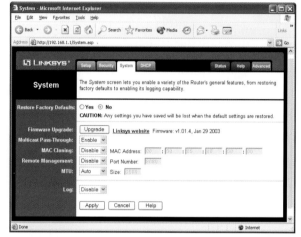

Remote management will allow you to change your router settings via the Internet.

A Log feature will keep track of all traffic on your Internet connection, similar to the ICF log file (see page 87).

MAC address cloning allows you to replace the MAC address of the router with another MAC address. Some ISP require you to register the MAC address of your computer and this feature allows your router to use this registered MAC address. If you need to use this feature follow these steps:

1. Find your computer's MAC address by typing ipconfig /all at the DOS command prompt (see page 151). The MAC address is the 12-digit "physical address" of the network adapter that is used for your Internet connection.

2. Select Enable from the drop down menu beside the MAC cloning option. The MAC address input field will now become active.

3. Enter the 12-digit MAC address of your network adapter into the field provided.

4. Click Apply to enable the revised settings.

DHCP Server Setup

Many routers can provide DHCP server functions, managing the assignment of IP addresses to computers in your network.

Although using DHCP is the easy option, manually assigning IP addresses gives an extra level of security in a wireless network.

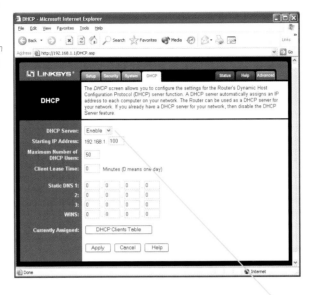

Make sure you only have one DHCP server enabled in your network!

I   To use the router's DHCP server click Enable. The default setting will generally not need to be changed.

2   Ensure that all PCs in your network are configured to obtain an IP address automatically. See page 97.

3   An option on this tab will allow you to view a list of IP addresses assigned by the DHCP server.

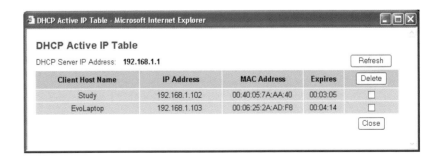

MAC Address Filtering

Advanced wireless options

Most of the advanced wireless settings can be left at their default values, but one option you may wish to use is MAC filtering. If you are running a community or neighborhood network you may wish to use this feature to restrict access to known users.

1 Select Enable from the drop down list against MAC filtering.

2 Select whether you want the access point to permit or prevent access for the MAC addresses in the filter list.

3 Enter the permitted or excluded MAC addresses in the filter list.

You'll need to ask each of your allowed users to find the MAC address of their wireless adapter using the ipconfig /all command at the DOS prompt.

Internet Filters

Most routers provide a range of filters that can be configured to block or enable particular kinds of Internet access.

For this router, up to 10 different access policies can be defined, each for a specified list of PCs.

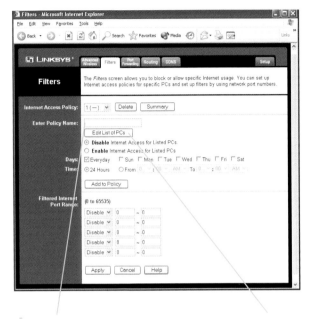

Enter a name for the access policy and list PCs to which this policy applies.

If you are using DHCP in your network you will have to identify PCs by their MAC addresses.

2 Specify the filters to be applied to this policy. Filtering on website URL, keyword and by access time or day of the week are typical options available.

3 Click Apply to update your access policies.

Advanced Options: Port Forwarding

You will need to configure this advanced option if any computer on your network is going to be acting as a web server, email server or ftp server.

Port Forwarding ensures that requests for these services are forwarded to the correct computer on your network.

If your ISP uses dynamic IP addressing you will need to use DDNS together with Port Forwarding. See page 108.

For each application requiring access through an external port you will need to enter the port range being used.

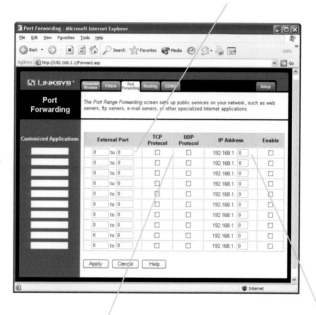

Information on the port ranges used will be in your application documentation.

Indicate which protocols are to be forwarded.

Any computer that is having a port forwarded must have a static IP address. DHCP must be disabled and the static IP address must be entered on the TCP/IP Properties, General tab. See page 97.

Enter the static IP address of the computer that is serving this application.

The documentation for your particular server application will give you further information on any specific requirements for that application.

Advanced Options: Routing

The routing functions of your hardware can be used in two modes, either as a gateway to the Internet, or as a router within a more complex network with other routers.

For most home and small office applications you will be using the gateway option.

1 Select the appropriate operating mode for your network; router or gateway.

2 You will have the option to build a static routing table to specify routing paths for network traffic, if you are skilled at network configuration.

With Dynamic Routing, a router will share its routing tables with others in response to RIP (Router Information Protocol) messages.

3 Router mode will include an option to use dynamic routing (RIP) which allows the router to build its own routing table.

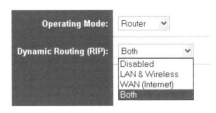

RIP will only be needed on the LAN/Wireless side if you have a very complex network!

4 Specify whether RIP is to be enabled on the WAN side of the router, the LAN/Wireless side or both.

Advanced Options: Dynamic Domain Name System

By combining DDNS and Port Forwarding (page 106) you will be able to direct calls from the Internet to a computer in your network even if your ISP uses DHCP.

If your ISP provides you with a dynamic IP address but you want your computer to run a server that can be accessed from the Internet, then you need a way for your visitors to find your server even when its IP address changes.

This can be achieved using a Dynamic Domain Name System (DDNS). Some gateways include this feature, but in order to use it you first need to register online with a DDNS service provider.

1 Register with a DDNS service such as www.tzo.com, www.dyndns.com or www.dynip.com.

2 Enable DDNS on your access point's DDNS configuration tab.

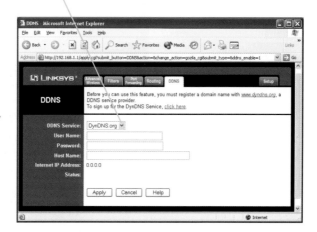

As here, you may have to select a specific DDNS service.

3 Enter the User Name, Password and Host Name from your DDNS service provider registration.

4 Click Apply to ensure that your updated settings are saved.

Wireless Network Security

In this chapter we look at wireless networking security, and you will learn how to ensure that your home or small office wireless network is safe against unwanted attention or access, for example from drive-by hackers (or nosey neighbors!).

Security features such as Wired Equivalent Privacy, MAC filtering and Virtual Private Networks will be covered, as well as the latest security upgrades available under Wi-Fi Protected Access (WPA).

Covers

Chapter Eight

What's at Stake?

Whether you're starting networking from scratch using wireless, or are upgrading an existing network with wireless components, you need to be aware that the great strength of wireless networking, namely its flexibility, is also a potential weakness.

Unlike a wired network, where you have to physically plug-in to gain access, wireless network traffic is broadcast on the air and is accessible to anyone with a wireless enabled PDA or computer.

War Driving

War driving takes its name from the movie "War Games", where hackers randomly dialed phone numbers until they found a modem.

This potential for easy access has inspired a movement known as "war driving", the practice of driving around with a wireless enabled laptop and an external antenna to identify and publicize the location of wireless networks.

A variant of this, "war chalking" emerged in London in 2002, with a set of symbols being chalked on sidewalks and buildings to identify access points.

let's warchalk..!	
KEY	SYMBOL
OPEN NODE	ssid X bandwidth
CLOSED NODE	ssid O
WEP NODE	ssid access contact W bandwidth
blackbeltjones.com/warchalking	

WEP vulnerability

In addition to the game of finding and accessing unsecured networks, the encryption method used in WEP was exposed early in its history as having cryptographic weaknesses.

Software to crack WEP can be downloaded free from the Internet!

The fact that the WEP encryption key stays unchanged unless manually reentered into every station in the network makes WEP vulnerable. WEP transmits information about the encrypting key as part of every data message and a determined hacker equipped with the necessary tools could collect and analyze transmitted data to extract the encrypting key.

This requires several million packets to be intercepted and analyzed, but could still be accomplished in under an hour on a high traffic network.

The latest version of 802.11 security (WPA) overcomes this vulnerability by providing for encryption keys to be changed automatically with time.

The type of security threats faced by a wireless network are many and varied, here are just a few:

Insertion attacks

An attacker is able to connect a wireless client to an access point without authorization because no password is requested.

Session hijacking

An attacker transmits false traffic into a connection and takes over the victim's TCP session.

Broadcast monitoring

In a poorly configured network, if the access point is connected to a hub rather than a switch, sensitive data packets not intended for wireless clients can be intercepted by an attacker.

ARP spoofing

An attacker can trick the network into routing sensitive data from a wired network onto the Internet, by accessing and corrupting routing tables.

Beware of any public hotspot that does not ask for your normal login information.
Disconnect immediately!

Evil twin intercept

An attacker uses an unauthorized access point to trick wireless clients to connect and reveal sensitive data such as passwords.

Denial of service attacks

"Popular" in wired networks, where an attacker floods a wireless client with bogus data packets.

Jamming

An attacker floods the 2.4GHz band with radio frequency interference, causing wireless communication to grind to a halt.

On a more mundane level, perhaps the worst that might happen is that you discover from your access log that the kid next door has been using your broadband Internet connection for free!

In most cases these types of attack require a high level of technical expertise on the part of the hacker, and they can be made that bit more difficult by ensuring that the full range of available security measures are enabled.

Wireless Security Best Practice

Wireless network security is seen as one of the main issues that is inhibiting wider uptake of the technology, and one that has resulted in a lot of critical press coverage.

If you want to provide free public access to an Internet connection your security measures will be different. See page 134.

The inherent vulnerability of the early 802.11b (Wi-Fi) security was recognized early on, but there are a number of steps that can be taken by anyone setting up a network that will give reasonable security against all but a determined hacker.

Change default SSID and disable SSID broadcast

See page 100 for an example of SSID disabling.

Wardrivers in the US report that about 60% of all access points broadcast with their default SSIDs and that less than 25% have enabled WEP. Changing the default and, if your access points allows it, disabling the SSID broadcast are the first steps that will protect your network from idle snoopers.

Use an administration password

Make sure that the setup function on your access point is password protected so that unauthorized users can not gain access and change the security settings.

Enable WEP

WPA and upgrading older gear to WPA are discussed in the following sections.

Enabling WEP, using hard to guess keys and changing them regularly are important security steps. WEP will be progressively replaced by WPA (see next section) following the ratification of the IEEE 802.11i standard.

MAC address filtering

MAC address filtering allows you to secure your wireless network by only allowing access to computers which have been registered on your access point.

A MAC or Media Access Control address is a 12 digit number that is unique to each network adapter.

MAC Address Filter List - Microsoft Internet Explorer

MAC Address Filter List

Enter MAC Address in this format: xxxxxxxxxxxx

Wireless Client MAC List

MAC 01:	MAC 11:
MAC 02:	MAC 12:
MAC 03:	MAC 13:

Use you AP's setup to enter allowed MAC addresses in the filter list. Keep the list up-to-date and delete any old entries.

Use a personal firewall

Ensure that you have a firewall installed and enabled as a security barrier. If your LAN and WLAN is connected to the Internet via a router then this is the place to install a firewall.

ICF was covered in chapter 6. Another product often recommended is Zone Alarm from www.zonelabs.com.

If you are using a laptop with a wireless adapter or built-in Wi-Fi to connect to a hotspot then enable the Windows XP ICF on your wireless network connection or install another product.

Consider manually assigning IP addresses

Although DHCP is easier to setup, manually assigning IP addresses to computers in your wireless network will prevent an unauthorized computer from obtaining an address automatically.

DHCP setup was covered on page 103. Select Disable if you want to assign IP addresses manually.

If you do decide to assign IP addresses manually, using a different set of private addresses rather than the default set for your access point will also keep would-be hackers guessing. For example the Linksys default set starts at 192.168.1.100. You can use any set in the private address ranges discussed on page 42.

Keep access points away from windows

Keeping your access point away from outside walls or windows will reduce the signal strength outside your home or office and limit the range at which unauthorized users might be able to detect and connect to your network.

Enable the log file and review access record regularly

Keeping a wireless access log will be one of the administrative functions of your access point. Enable the log and review its contents regularly to make sure any unauthorized access is identified.

Installing firmware updates may result in setting reverting to factory default values.

Keep firmware up-to-date

Finally, as the manufacturer of your network gear releases updated firmware and device drivers, download and install these so that your system is fully up-to-date with any security updates.

Disable your wireless adapter when not in use

While your wireless network adapter is enabled, Windows XP will be constantly on the look out for an access point or ad hoc connection matching one of the preferred network profiles you have defined.

It is possible for a hacker to set up a rogue access point matching one of your hotspot profiles. Disabling your adapter when you don't intend to connect will prevent attack by this route.

If the icon is displayed in your notification area you can also right click this to access your network adapter.

1 Access your network adapter by opening the Network Connections folder from the Start menu or from your desktop icon.

2 Right click on the Wireless Connection and select Disable.

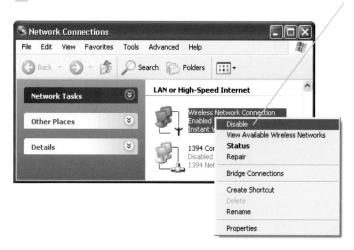

3 When you want to use the wireless adapter again repeat these steps and select Enable.

Wi-Fi Protected Access (WPA)

Wi-Fi Protected Access, or WPA, has been developed to overcome the known shortcomings in WEP described earlier. WPA is specified in the IEEE 802.11i standard that was ratified in June 2003 and provides new security features in five key areas.

Temporal Key Integrity Protocol (TKIP)

Encryption is mandatory under WPA, rather than optional as was the case for earlier 802.11 standards. TKIP changes the encryption keys and manages the synchronization of changing keys across the wireless network.

Michael

WPA improves previous integrity checks with a new 8-byte Message Integrity Code (the MIC in Michael). This is used to confirm that the data in a transmitted frame has not been tampered with.

Advanced Encryption Standard (AES)

Versions of WEP up to 256-bit are offered by some vendors, but these are not part of a standard and there is no certification of interoperability. In fact the longer keys give no significant additional protection.

AES replaces the WEP encryption with a new algorithm that uses 128-, 192- or 256-bit keys, compared to the 40-bit original WEP keys.

AES is optional within the new standard. This is because WPA is intended to be backwards compatible with earlier 802.11 devices but the new algorithm requires a new chip set and cannot be implemented as part of a firmware upgrade.

User authentication

As WPA becomes widely adopted we will probably see authentication servers being added to the ever growing list of access point capabilities.

Authentication of users was optional for previous 802.11 versions but is required under WPA. Authentication can be via a pre-shared key or, for larger networks, WPA supports the use of a dedicated authentication server.

Installing WPA

Although full implementation of WPA, with certified interoperability has to await new hardware releases, many of the features can be implemented by installing free firmware upgrades to existing equipment.

An update to Windows XP may also be required, as described in the next section.

Updating Windows XP for WPA

To install the WPA update, your Windows XP must be upgraded with the Service Pack 1 updates. To update your XP version to SP1 level see page 118. If your XP version is at SP2 level, WPA will already be installed and you can skip this section.

An update to Windows XP to enable Wi-Fi Protected Access is available as a free download from the Microsoft Support website at http://support.microsoft.com/?kbid=815485.

An additional security feature of the SP1/WPA upgrades is that Windows XP will warn you and ask for positive confirmation if you're about to connect to a wireless network on which WEP is not enabled.

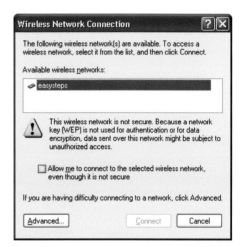

Downloading and installing the WPA update

1 Start up Internet Explorer and type the above URL into the address field. The WPA upgrade overview article will load.

2 Scroll down through the article and click the link to access the WPA update program.

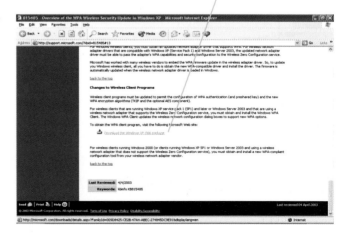

3 Click Download to start the download process.

4 Click Save to save the update file on your computer for later installation.

5 Select a location, on your Desktop or in My Documents, to save the update file to.

HOT TIP

If you get an error message saying that the version of the Service Pack on your system is lower than necessary to apply the update, then follow the steps on page 118 to download and install the appropriate Service Pack.

6 When you are ready to run the update, double click the file on your Desktop or in My Documents.

Q815485_WXP
_SP2_x86_ENU

Updating Windows XP with Service Pack 1 Updates

To check the update level of your Windows XP version click Start, Control Panel, System and the Service Pack level is indicated on the General tab.

Windows updates are issued as Service Packs. In order to upgrade your wireless security to the WPA standard your Windows XP version must be at least up to the SP1 update level.

Besides enabling the WPA updates, updating your version of Windows XP with Service Pack 1 will also include the latest updates for other Windows XP security issues and application compatibility, as well as improving operating system reliability.

Obtaining Windows XP Service Pack 1 updates

Open your Internet browser and go to the Microsoft support website at http://support.microsoft.com/default.aspx?scid=kb;en-us;q322389.

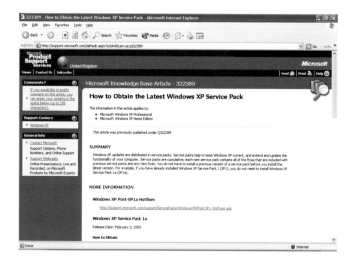

2 From this website you can either download the SP1 updates and apply them directly, save them to disk for later installation, or order a free CD containing the updates. The download file is several MB, so if your Internet connection is not broadband you may want to use the CD option.

If you have taken the CD route rather than downloading the update files, applying the updates is very straightforward.

Installing Service Pack 1 updates

Shut down all other programs before installing the SP1 update.

Insert the SP1 CD into your CD-ROM drive. Windows XP will recognize the disc and display the welcome page. Scroll down to the Install Service Pack 1 section and click the link to install SP1.

When prompted, click Open to run the XPSP1.CMD file.

The Windows XP Service Pack 1 Setup Wizard will start. After shutting down all programs, click Next to continue.

To retain the option to revert to a pre-SP1 version of your operating system select Archive files. Click Next to continue.

The setup wizard will check for available disk space before archiving files. If you don't have sufficient free space on your hard drive you will not be able to archive files.

There is a point of no return in the installation process when the Cancel button will become inactive and you will have to wait for the process to complete.

If you have selected the Archive option, the SP1 setup wizard will archive the relevant system files and install the updated files.

When the update is completed you will have the option to restart automatically on Finish or to delay and restart later.

Once the SP1 update is completed you will be able to install the Wi-Fi Protected Access updates, as described on page 116.

Updating Wireless Adapter Drivers for WPA

Until wireless gear starts shipping with WPA included, or if you want to upgrade existing gear to enable WPA, updated firmware or drivers can be downloaded from the manufacturers' websites for their most popular hardware components.

WPA upgrade for Linksys WPC11 wireless adapter

Web sites for other manufacturers will be different. There may be a specific download page for all products.

1 On the Linksys website at www.linksys.com, navigate to the WPC11 product page via Products, Wireless, Network Adapters. Click Drivers and Downloads.

2 Click the link to start the updated driver download.

This download is over 9MB. Some manufacturers may offer a free upgrade CD for customers who don't have a broadband Internet connection.

3 When prompted by Windows XP select Save, and in the next dialog box specify a location to save the file to on your computer.

4 The new firmware will be downloaded and saved to the location you specified.

Installing the driver upgrade

1 Open Network Connections, right click on your wireless network connection and click Properties.

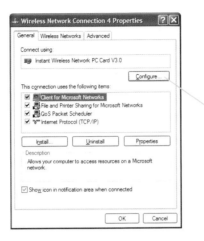

2 On the General tab click Configure.

3 In the Properties dialog box for your wireless adapter select the Driver tab.

4 Click Update Driver... and the Hardware Update Wizard will start.

5 Select Install from a list or specific location and click Next.

6 Select Search for the best drivers in these locations and Include this location in the search.

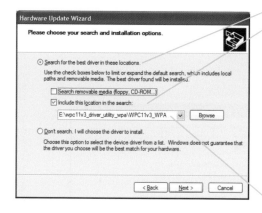

7 Navigate to the folder containing the downloaded driver and click Next.

8 The wizard will locate the new driver and begin the update. Click Finish to complete the update.

Windows XP may warn you that the software has not passed Windows XP Logo testing. Click Continue anyway to go ahead with the update.

Extending Wireless Network Range

In this chapter we'll take a look at extending the range of your wireless network beyond your home or small office.

You'll learn about using external antennas to increase your range and about ways to connect two wireless networks together. We'll also cover community wireless and the opportunity to set yourself up as a wireless ISP.

Covers

Chapter Nine

Why Worry About Range?

So far you've probably not been bothered by the question of the range of your wireless network – surfing the Internet from a coffee shop hotspot, or sharing files between computers in your home is not going to be an issue (unless you live in a mansion!).

But if the only seat in the departure lounge is in an area of low signal strength, or you want to share your broadband Internet connection with your neighbors, either as a free service to your community or as a commercial venture, then getting the most out of every milliwatt of transmitted power is going to be important to you.

The limit for the 2.4GHz ISM band used by 802.11b gear is 200mW (in USA) or 100mW (in UK) of "equivalent isotropically radiated power" or EIRP (see chapter 13).

In every country, national agencies specify the maximum power that can be transmitted in any radio frequency band, so it's not just a case of getting a more powerful transmitter.

Within the set limits, getting maximum range comes down to using a high gain antenna to increase your receiving sensitivity and to get your transmitted signal out as far as possible.

Antenna Basics

The two key characteristics of an antenna that you need to know about are its gain and radiation pattern.

Gain is a measure of how well the antenna increases effective signal power, and is measured in decibel units (dB). A convenient rule of thumb is to remember that 3dB represents a doubling of power. Typical gains for Wi-Fi antennas are in the range of 3dB to 20dB.

The radiation pattern of an antenna tells you how much power goes in various directions relative to the antenna axis. The simplest antenna, radiating equally in all directions, has a so-called isotropic radiation pattern resembling the shape of a baseball.

Antenna manufacturers usually specify gain in dBi, which is dB relative to an isotropic antenna.

The highest gain antennas radiate energy predominantly in one direction and have a radiation pattern resembling a spotlight or baseball bat.

Making the Most of What You've Got

There are some simple steps you can take before resorting to external antennas in order to get the best possible range from your current transmitter power and receiver sensitivity.

Avoiding Obstacles

Out of doors, trees are a major problem, but only when they are in leaf!

1 Moving your access point away from a wall, or raising it higher off the ground will improve its propagation pattern.

2 Metal objects such as filing cabinets, furniture or shelving can also attenuate radio waves. Try to keep access points and receivers away from large metal objects.

Adjust Access Point antennas

This is just like adjusting your TV aerial to get the best possible reception.

1 The signal strength from most access points will not be the same in all directions. Try adjusting the orientation of you AP and see if this improves signal strength at your receiver.

2 If your AP has two adjustable "rabbit ear" antennas try aligning one antenna vertically and the other horizontally.

Reorient your laptop

The transmitting power and receiving sensitivity of your wireless network adapter will also be strongest in one plane or direction. Changing the orientation of the adapter, either by facing in a different direction or by tilting at an angle can give you better signal strength.

Use an antenna enhancer

Some designs for antenna enhancers can be found at www.freeantennas. com.

If these steps don't give you the range you need, try an antenna enhancer, which improves antenna gain by adding a reflecting surface to the existing antenna on an access point.

Using an External Antenna to Increase Range

If extending the range is going to be important to you then you need to make sure when you buy your wireless gear that it allows you to connect an external antenna. This means either removable antennas in the case of an access point or a miniature connector in the case of a PC or PCMCIA card.

Several different types of antenna are available on the market, and the choice will depend on whether you want to increase sensitivity over a wide area or focus your transmitted power into a narrow beam in order to achieve maximum range in just one direction.

We'll look at the options starting with wide beamwidth and narrowing down.

Omnidirectional Antennas

An omnidirectional antenna such as the Buffalo WLE-NDR has a gain of 2.5dBi and a radiation pattern resembling a flat doughnut. It will increase your range over a wide area horizontally by reducing the amount of transmitted energy radiated vertically.

A 3dB gain gives a doubling of power at the receiver.

Patch Antennas

The patch antenna is more focused than the omni, with a forward pointing beamwidth of around 75 degrees. The Buffalo WLE-DA is an example of a patch antenna with a gain of 4dBi.

Directional Antennas

No, its not a sawn-off light sabre! Inside the protective housing is a directional yagi antenna of the type that can give you maximum range and minimum beamwidth. The Buffalo WLE-HG-DYG shown here will give you a gain of 14dBi (25 times the power compared to an

In the UK, the RA limits relate to power transmitted at the antenna, so if your transmitter is already close to the limit a high gain antenna can take you over the top. Check out EIRP in chapter 13 to make sure you stay legal. In the USA, the FCC allows an increase in EIRP for high gain antennas, since their narrow beamwidth means they will cause less spurious interference. Sadly the regulations are not so lenient in the UK!

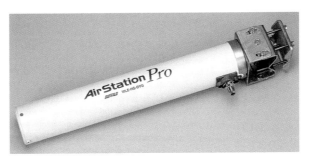

isotropic antenna). This type of antenna is best suited to point-to-point applications, for example if you want to bridge between buildings or more remote locations. Parabolic antennas, like the common satellite dish, can achieve even higher gain and narrower radiation pattern than the yagi.

Connecting to a PC card

To connect an external antenna to a wireless adapter in a laptop you will need an adapter cable to convert from the connector on the PC card to the type-N or BNC connector on the antenna. An example of the type of connector is the Buffalo WLE-LNC illustrated here.

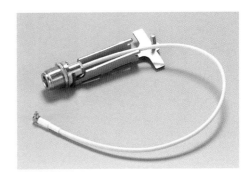

Do-It-Yourself Antennas

Wireless networking may still be new technology, but it's quickly developing a folklore all its own, and a large part of that relates to the area of DIY antennas. This famously started with an antenna made by wireless networking pioneer Rob Flickenger from a Pringles can plus a few bits and pieces from the garage.

Commercial antennas are not particularly expensive but if you have a practical bent and get a kick out of a string and sealing wax approach to high tech this might be an interesting way to spend a spare evening.

Here are a few of the best sources of information.

The Original Pringles Can Antenna

You can read all about Rob Flickenger's original Pringles can antenna at www.oreillynet.com/cs/weblog/view/wlg/448.

Lincomatic's Homebrew Wi-Fi Antenna Site

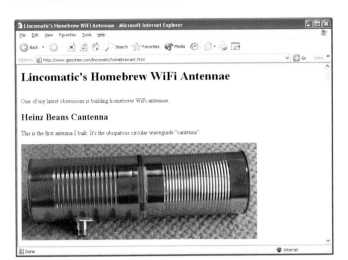

Lincomatic's Homebrew Antenna site shows examples of a range of DIY antennas, including omnidirectional and patch designs, as well as the cantenna shown above. You can find this site at www.geocities.com/lincomatic/homebrewant.html.

The Double Quad and Patch designs are particularly effective and easy to build. The Patch is small enough to pop in your laptop case and can give you an added boost at a hotspot if you're just a little out of range.

Another website worth taking a look at is http://www.netscum.com/~clapp/wireless.html.

Antenna Enhancers

As an alternative to a DIY antenna, an antenna enhancer adds a reflecting surface to the existing antenna on an access point for example, to enhance the antenna gain. Some designs for enhancers can be found at www.freeantennas.com.

Wireless Network Bridging

Connecting two physically separated networks using a wireless link is called wireless bridging. Most access points can also function as wireless bridges, and you can also buy dedicated devices that work as bridges only, connecting to similar devices but not to client computers.

Point to point mode

The simplest wireless bridge is a point to point connection between two wired LANs. This might be a solution if you have wired LANs in two nearby buildings that you want to connect without running an Ethernet cable between them.

Directional high gain antennas will give a big boost to a point to point connection.

Point to multipoint mode

To connect more than two nearby wired LANs you will need to use point to multipoint mode, where one access point or bridge is working as a central hub to route traffic between the other access points.

One AP should be configured in point to multipoint mode. The other APs should be in point to point mode. One AP is operating as a hub for the others.

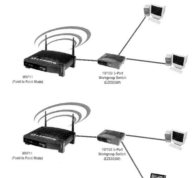

If you also want to connect individual computers wirelessly to any of the LANs you will need a separate access point for that LAN, since an access point in bridge mode cannot also work as a normal access point connecting to wireless clients.

The exception to this is access point client mode which is an operating mode available in some vendor's access points.

Access point client mode

In this mode the MAC address of the main AP is entered into the client AP setup.

This mode allows you to extend the range of your wireless network by linking one access point to another, while each AP is also hosting other wireless clients in an infrastructure mode network.

Interoperability is likely to be an issue with access point bridging modes. Stick to one manufacturer unless you are able to experiment before buying.

Last mile Internet access

One important application of wireless bridging is in extending the coverage of broadband Internet in areas where this is currently limited.

For example, a small community which is just out of range of a DSL enabled phone exchange, could gain broadband Internet access by wireless bridging to a LAN which is connected to the exchange.

Or an expensive satellite broadband connection could be shared across a community by bridging several WLANs together. Community wireless and setting up a wireless ISP are covered in the next sections.

Community Wireless

In the UK a company called SkyLinc is planning to use helium filled balloons, tethered a mile above ground, as base stations to beam broadband Internet access to areas such as rural communities where DSL or cable services are not available.

Interest in community wireless has been a major factor in the rapid growth in sales of Wi-Fi gear over the last few years. Wireless networking provides an inexpensive means of providing broadband Internet access to a community where a wired network would be impractical.

Community wireless projects are springing up around the globe, from Seattle and Somerset to Singapore and Sydney. There is a wealth of information on the Internet, including a helpful Get Started guide on the SeattleWireless.net site.

Setting up a community wireless project

1. Before you start, check the small print of your ISP agreement to make sure that sharing your broadband connection is permitted. If sharing is not mentioned check with your ISP and if you find it's not allowed then try shopping around for a more community friendly provider!

2. The first step is to see whether your community shares your interest in wireless networking. Print some posters for local shops, libraries and schools. Drop some flyers into mail boxes and email your local radio, TV and newspapers to gauge the level of interest.

An external omnidirectional antenna with a few dB gain will extend this a little.

Microwave propagation programs are available which can check the suitability of antenna sites using local terrain maps.

If your site owners want to charge a rent then you'll have to factor this in to your overall project costs.

You'll find sample constitutions and antenna site owner agreements on the Internet, for example at www.wlan.org.uk.

3 Based on the response you receive you need to establish the area you want to try to cover with your community wireless network. The advertised open air range of an access point will be in the range of 1000 to 1500 feet. Choose a conservative figure and map out how many access points you need to cover your target area.

4 Walk around your community and identify suitable sites for your external antennas. The main criterion is good line-of-site visibility to your target area but a remote hill top may not be ideal as you'll also need a power connection.

5 Consider the wireless bridging options covered in the previous section if your target area extends beyond the range of a single access point.

6 Talk to the (hopefully community spirited) owners of the sites where you'd like to put your antennas and get their OK.

7 Next do the sums! Plan and cost all the gear you need for the project, plus any rents and broadband Internet costs. Share these setup and ongoing costs information with your community group and agree how these costs are going to be covered.

8 Setting up a constitution for the group may seem unnecessarily formal, but will provide a clear and agreed basis for resolving any later disputes.

9 Order and install your access points and antennas, and assist users with wireless adapter installation and setup.

10 Test all equipment on-site. Check wireless coverage with a wireless enabled laptop or PDA. The Netstumbler program, available from www.netstumbler.com has a useful signal to noise readout for checking wireless signal strength.

Hold your official opening. Secure the services of a local celebrity and get plenty of publicity from local media.

Security for community wireless projects

Many of the security issues for a community wireless project will be similar to those for a private infrastructure mode wireless network as we discussed in chapter 8.

The key issue that your group will need to decide is whether the service is limited to payed-up members, or whether, once the basic setup and running costs are covered, other users within the community will be allowed free access.

Members only: If your group decides to keep the shared service closed, then all the security measures discussed in chapter 8 can be applied; disabling SSID broadcast, enabling WEP, registering the MAC addresses of members, etc.

In addition, every member should enable firewall software either using the Windows XP ICF or another firewall product, in order to protect themselves from unwanted attention from the Internet.

Open access service: On the other hand, if your group decides to allow free access to anyone in the community, these security measures will not be applied. You will want to broadcast the SSID and disable WEP, MAC address filtering, etc.

You may want to change the SSID to reflect the name of your community project.

The firewall issue remains, and as organizer of the group it will be helpful to advise and assist other users in setting up this feature.

Community wireless administration

Whichever model your group chooses, you should ensure that the access point administration function is secure by setting an administrative password.

As well as Internet connection sharing, IP telephony might be an interesting service to consider as part of a community project. See page 158.

Enabling the log file and regularly reviewing the log file records will also give you a good idea of network usage, and alert you to any unauthorized access if you're running a members only service.

Set Up Your Own Wireless ISP (WISP)

Running your own commercial hotspot may be a viable alternative to offering wireless Internet access as a free service in your community.

Your home may be located next to a park or other venue where people want to connect to the Internet, or you may already run a venue, such as a coffee shop or bookstore, and want to offer Internet access to customers to encourage trade.

Alternatively you might be right on the edge of the area of DSL coverage from your local phone exchange and be able to sell-on a DSL service via a wireless "last mile" connection to those just outside the land line coverage.

Technical setup

A free access service won't need to worry about security measures like WEP. But if your own computer is connected to the AP, wirelessly or via a LAN, make sure your firewall is enabled or you may find your customers browsing the business accounts!

Whatever your business purpose, the technical steps we covered in the last section for setting up a community project are still relevant. Follow these steps to sort out the physical aspects of your WISP.

If you're setting up your WISP in a venue like a coffee shop or bookstore, you won't need to worry about external antennas. Locate your access point in a prominent unobstructed position where it will not interfere with business or be interfered with by microwave ovens or large appliances like the espresso machine.

RF propagation at 2.5 GHz needs a line of sight from transmitter to receiver or signal strength (and transmitted data rate) will drop off rapidly.

If you're setting up a "last mile" service you might also want to think about combining external antennas with some of the bridging options we looked at on page 130–131. These may help you to get around obstructions like unhelpfully placed hills or buildings.

Commercial setup

A bigger challenge in setting up your service will be on the commercial side. If you want to run your WISP as a business venture rather than as a customer incentive then how are you going to collect your revenue? There are a number of options open to you:

> Advertise in local papers and shops for interest in your project, particularly if you're aiming to set up a "last mile" service.

2   Sign up interested customers to your service, either informally or with the aid of a simple customer agreement. Google will probably turn up numerous examples on the Internet.

3   If you don't want to go it alone, sign up with one of the virtual hotspot networks. In the USA check out Boingo, Pronto, NetNearU, FatPort, iPass and about a hundred others.

In the UK, virtual networks are just starting up. Check out My Zones or The Cloud (coming soon!), as well as Boingo.

Internationally, Boingo operates in over 12 countries. As well as the USA and the UK, it's in Australia, Canada and the Netherlands. Or search in the hotspot directories (see page 164) to find virtual networks operating in your location.

4   Finally, if you're feeling really entrepreneurial, how about starting your own virtual network? Maybe your start-up can grow to become the next big international name in virtual networks.

Network Troubleshooting

Despite following all the steps in the previous chapters it's only a matter of time before you hit the unexpected.

In this chapter we'll start troubleshooting by trying to pin down the source of the problem. Then we'll cover problem symptoms you may encounter and possible solutions. Finally we'll look at the network diagnostic tools available in Windows XP and in MS DOS.

Covers

Chapter Ten

First Analyze the Problem

The first step in troubleshooting any networking problems is to use some common sense to try to track down the cause of the problem.

For example, if you are trying to access a file on another computer in your network, then for this to work you must have:

A working connection means both the physical link works (e.g. not using a crossover cable when a straight through is needed) and that the software works (e.g. that the necessary protocols are installed).

You may find it helpful to make a sketch of your network connection then check off each element as you confirm that it's working properly. Don't forget the software as well as hardware!

- a network adapter, properly installed and configured in your computer,

- a working connection to your network hardware such as a hub, switch or access point,

- a working connection from this hardware to the other networked computer,

- a properly installed and configured network adapter in the other computer,

- the file you're trying to access needs to be enabled for sharing.

Troubleshooting process

If you are unable to reach any resources on your network then the problem may be with your network adapter or its configuration. You may get this kind of message:

With a wireless network you may still get this message for a few seconds after making the wireless connection. Try again after a few seconds.

Start with the section Troubleshooting Network Adapters on page 140. Come back to step 2 if your adapter checks out OK.

2 Use the DOS "ping" command to do a loopback check on your network adapter. See the section Checking Network Connectivity on page 148 to learn how to do this.

3   If your adapter seems OK, then the next thing to check is network connectivity. You may get this kind of warning if your connection is down.

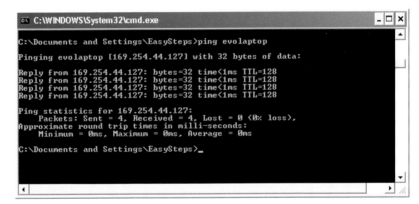

Use the DOS ipconfig command to check that your computer has a valid IP address assigned to it. See the section Other DOS Diagnostic Tools on page 151 to learn about ipconfig.

Use the ipconfig command to find the address of another computer, or use your default gateway IP address to ping your Internet gateway.

4   Check that your computer can "ping" other devices on the network. See the section Checking Network Connectivity on page 148 to learn how to do this.

Take a look at Troubleshooting Network Connections on page 143 if it looks like this might be the problem area.

It will also help your diagnosis if you can check whether other computers on the network have a similar problem accessing the network resource.

5   If your computer and network connection seem OK then perform the same checks from the computer you are trying to reach, to ensure that its adapter and connection are working.

If these steps do not identify the problem, check out the MS Help and Support Center on page 153, or the troubleshooting websites on page 170.

Troubleshooting Network Adapters

If it looks like the problem is with a particular network device check its physical installation, its configuration and then run the Windows Hardware Device Troubleshooter.

Check the physical installation

 If the connection that you are troubleshooting is not in Network Connections, the adapter may be disconnected, for example if it's a USB device.

1 Check that the device is correctly inserted or plugged in, powered up (if applicable), and that any necessary cables are also properly plugged in.

2 Open Network Connections. Check that the network connection is not disabled or disconnected.

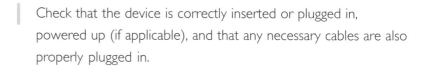

 If an adapter has been switched off or ejected from its PC slot it may be necessary to restart the computer to get the adapter to restart correctly.

3 If the device is disabled, right click the connection icon and click Enable.

Check the device configuration

1 Double click the network connection that you're troubleshooting.

2 On the General tab, check that all the needed items are installed.

See page 38 to install any missing items.

3 Click Configure in the Properties dialog box for this connection. The Properties dialog box for the adapter will open.

It's worthwhile checking on the manufacturer's website to make sure you have the latest version of the driver and firmware for your adapter.

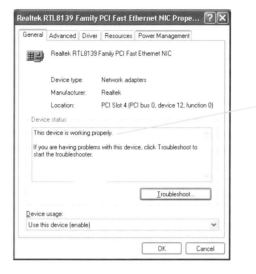

The device Properties box will indicate whether the device is working properly.

4 If the device is not working properly click Troubleshoot... to start the Hardware Device Troubleshooter.

If your hardware comes with a manufacturer's diagnostic program you can also use this to test the device.

If none of these checks reveal the problem you could also try removing it and reinstalling it, connecting it to another computer, checking the manufacturer's website for any driver updates/compatibility issues, or searching websites on page 170.

Troubleshooting Network Resource Hosts

On the computer that's hosting the resource you're trying to reach, you should also check that the network adapter is properly installed and configured.

1   Check that the host computer is switched on and its network adapter is enabled. Open Network Connections on the host computer and check the status of the network link from both ends.

If one or other computer has been switched off and on again, interrupting a wireless link, try switching off both computers and restarting. The wireless link should reestablish itself automatically.

2   If the configuration of the host computer's network adapter has been changed since the connection was last established, other computers in the workgroup may need to be configured to match.

3   For a wireless network, if WEP enablement has been changed on one computer, network communications will not work and you will not be able to "ping" another computer. Follow the steps at the end of chapter 5 (page 78) to update WEP on other computers in the network.

4   Confirm that the sharing status of the file, directory or other resource has not been changed since the last time it was accessed (see chapter 3, page 34).

Shared Music

5   Check that the target file or directory has not been moved since the Network Place was set up. Windows gives a warning if an attempt is made to move a shared file or directory.

If you are unable to see a computer that was previously accessible as part of your workgroup then as a last resort rerun the network setup wizard and redefine your workgroup (see page 24).

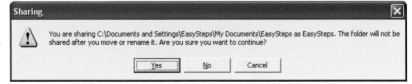

Sharing

You are sharing C:\Documents and Settings\EasySteps\My Documents\EasySteps as EasySteps. The folder will not be shared after you move or rename it. Are you sure you want to continue?

Yes   No   Cancel

Troubleshooting Network Connections

If your network adapter checks out, the next thing to verify is the physical link to your network hub, switch or access point.

If you have any crossover cables in your toolbox make sure you use them for hub-to-hub or computer-to-computer links only.

1 Check that cables are properly connected and do not show any physical damage. If possible test a suspect cable in another part of the network.

2 If you suspect a hub or switch is the problem, try connecting the two computers directly with a crossover cable. If this works then you've probably discovered the source of the problem.

If you are in the habit of disabling your wireless adapter when not in use check that the adapter is enabled when you are ready to use the wireless link again.

3 In wireless networks, verify that the connection parameters such as the SSID have not been changed on either the host or remote computer, or on the access point.

4 Similarly for an ad hoc connection, verify that the properties for the connection are identical at both ends. Make sure that if WEP is enabled, the check box for "The key is provided for me automatically" is unchecked.

You will have a different format for this dialog box if you have updated your Windows XP with the SP1/WPA upgrades (see page 116).

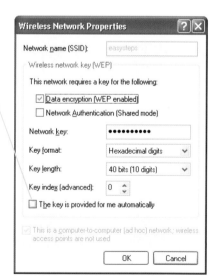

If the View Available Wireless Networks dialog box is grayed out check out page 146.

5 If a wireless connection is intermittent, check for any sources of interference (see page 144) or try moving closer to the access point or to the other computer in an ad hoc network.

Wireless Interference

The 2.4GHz ISM band used for Wi-Fi communications is also used by a wide variety of other devices, from microwave ovens to garage door remote controllers and cordless phones.

Bluetooth wireless devices also use the 2.4GHz band and will cause performance degradation in the vicinity of a Wi-Fi network. The IEEE 802.11 and 802.15 standards groups are working to alleviate this problem.

If you experience reduced data speed on your wireless connection, or hear pops and crackles on your cordless phone it could be due to interference between different devices.

The so-called "collision avoidance" algorithm used for WI-Fi (see CSMA/CA in chapter 13) means that interference will not cause you to lose data, but it will cause lots of data frames to have to be retransmitted, slowing down transfer rates.

Try any or all of the following steps to minimize or eliminate interference.

Interference with cordless phones

1 Check to see whether your phone is a Frequency Hopping or Direct Sequence device (check out these terms in chapter 13.)

2 If it's a Direct Sequence device, try operating your access point or ad hoc link on another channel. Try channels 1 or 11 at either end of the ISM band.

Keep your access point at least 10 feet away from a microwave oven.

3 Change the position of your access point, or of the cordless phone base station. Try to maximize the separation between these devices.

4 If you have the option, connect an external antenna to the wireless network adapter. A high gain antenna with a narrow beamwidth is less sensitive to interfering signals coming from outside its radiation pattern.

5 If none of these measures are effective then junk the cordless phone, try to get one that operates on another frequency band, or consider upgrading your wireless LAN to 802.11g on the 5 GHz band.

Troubleshooting Internet Connection Sharing

If Internet Connection Sharing (ICS) has been enabled (see chapter 6 page 82) but you are unable to control the connection from a network computer, check the ICS setup.

Unable to remotely control an Internet connection

You may also find that the Internet Gateway icon is no longer present in the Network Connections folder, despite network control of the connection being previously enabled.

If ICS control by network computers was previously enabled on the host computer's settings for the dial up connection, but the above warning is displayed when trying to control the connection:

1. Check that network control of the connection has not been disabled on the host computer. On the host computer open

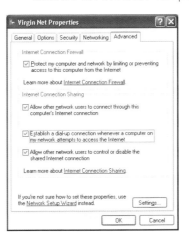

Network Connections, right click the icon for your dial up Internet connection, select Properties and Advanced. Ensure that the Allow other network users... check box is checked and click OK.

2. If the checkbox was unchecked in step 1 then try again to control the Internet connection from the network computer, otherwise try restarting the ICS host computer.

Wireless Zero Configuration is Not Accessible

The option to View Available Wireless Networks comes up when you right click the Windows XP Zero Configuration icon in the notification area.

When trying to connect to a wireless network using Windows XP Wireless Zero Configuration, after selecting View Available Wireless Networks, you may find that the Connect to Wireless Network dialog box is grayed out and inactive.

This will occur if the Wireless Zero Configuration service has been turned off. Follow the following steps to restore the service.

The Wireless Zero Configuration Service is a piece of software that Windows needs in order to create new wireless connections.

Right click My Computer on your desktop and select Manage

2 Expand Services and Applications and then double click Services

3 Scroll down the services list to Wireless Zero Configuration and double click this line.

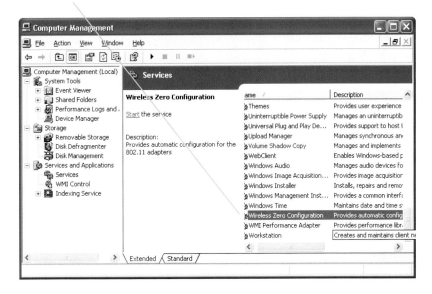

4 In the Wireless Zero Configuration dialog box click Start and Windows XP will restart the service.

The Connect to Wireless Network dialog box will now be active and you will be able to select the network you want to connect to.

Checking Network Connectivity

If you have trouble reaching another computer on your network, the place to start is to check that all the plugs, cables and removable network adapters are properly installed.

A problem with wired network connections may be indicated in Network Connections as shown here, where a disconnected network cable is indicated.

You will also see this icon if you are using a crossover cable instead of a straight through cable or if the device at the other end of the cable is switched off.

If all the cables check out then there are a number of tools available to test your network interface card (NIC) and its connectivity across the network to other computers.

Checking your NIC using the Ping test

Ping tests network connectivity by sending a data packet called an echo request to the indicated IP address and timing the echo response.

1 Open a DOS prompt window by clicking Start, Run. Type "cmd" in the Open field and click OK.

This IP address (127.0.0.1) is a reserved address that points to the NIC on the host computer. Testing the NIC in this way is called a loopback test. You can also type ping localhost or ping name, where name is the name you gave to the computer you are checking when you set up your network.

2 In the DOS prompt window type ping 127.0.0.1

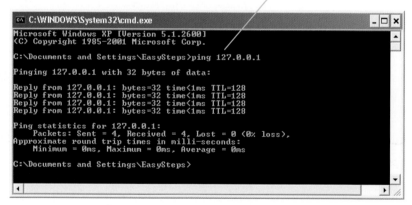

3 Four echo request packets are sent and the return times are shown if the test is successful. If you get the message "Request timed out" the NIC is not responding to the echo requests.

If your network interface card passes the loopback test the next step is to check connectivity to other computers on your network. The ping test will do this for you too.

To ping another computer you need to know the computer's IP address. If the computer is in your local network you can also use the computer name.

Pinging another computer

You can also find the IP address of a computer from the DOS prompt by typing ipconfig /all.

Notice that the IP address here is allocated by the Windows XP Automatic Private IP Addressing service (APIPA). See page 41.

To find the IP address of a computer open Network Connections, right click the Local Area or Wireless Network connection and expand the Details section on the task pane. The IP address is shown here.

Open the DOS prompt window as described on the last page. Type "ping IP address", where IP address is the address of the computer you want to test connectivity to.

You can also ping the name of the computer if it is in your local network. Here the computer is pinged using the command >ping evolaptop.

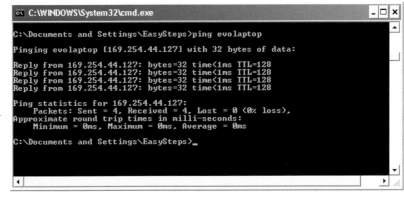

Here the connectivity check to the target computer was successful.

Diagnosing unsuccessful ping tests

A "Request timed out" or a "Destination host unreachable" message indicates that the ping test to a remote computer was not successful.

"Request timed out" indicates that the echo request packets were sent out but no response was received. The problem may be with the remote computer:

IP addressing will not be a problem if the APIPA service is used.

- IP address is incorrect,

- computer is off or has crashed,

- NIC is not working properly,

- computer has a firewall enabled on this connection.

It is not advised to enable a firewall such as ICF on internal network connection, only on the connection to the Internet at an ICS host or Internet gateway.

The problem may also be with the host computer or elsewhere in the network:

- host computer has incorrect IP address or subnet mask,

- an interconnecting hub or switch is not working.

A "Destination host unreachable" message indicates that the host computer or some intermediate routing device is unable to contact the remote computer. This may be due to:

- host computer is disconnected from the network,

- your router is disconnected from the network,

- an intervening router is disconnected.

There are a number of options that you can use with the ping command to gather more information. To see these options just type ping in the DOS prompt window without an IP address.

The problem may also indicate that a router does not have any information on how to route traffic to the address that you are trying to ping.

Other DOS Diagnostic Tools

There are a number of other tools that can be invoked from the DOS prompt that can help you trace any problems with network connectivity.

Ipconfig

Ipconfig gives you the basic IP configuration information for all the network adapters connected to your computer.

```
Command Prompt                                                  - □ ×
Microsoft Windows XP [Version 5.1.2600]
(C) Copyright 1985-2001 Microsoft Corp.

C:\Documents and Settings\EasySteps>ipconfig

Windows IP Configuration

Ethernet adapter Local Area Connection 2:

        Media State . . . . . . . . . . . : Media disconnected

Ethernet adapter Wireless Network Connection:

        Connection-specific DNS Suffix  . :
        Autoconfiguration IP Address. . . : 169.254.186.233
        Subnet Mask . . . . . . . . . . . : 255.255.0.0
        Default Gateway . . . . . . . . . :
```

Type ipconfig /? at the DOS prompt to see the full list of command options.

The option "ipconfig /all" gives you further detailed configuration information on your NICs, such as MAC addresses, DHCP status, etc., as well as host configuration information.

Some ipconfig command options can disrupt your network connection – for example by releasing automatically assigned IP addresses. Take care here!

```
Command Prompt                                                  - □ ×
C:\Documents and Settings\EasySteps>ipconfig /all

Windows IP Configuration

        Host Name . . . . . . . . . . . . : Study
        Primary Dns Suffix  . . . . . . . :
        Node Type . . . . . . . . . . . . : Unknown
        IP Routing Enabled. . . . . . . . : Yes
        WINS Proxy Enabled. . . . . . . . : Yes

Ethernet adapter Local Area Connection 2:

        Connection-specific DNS Suffix  . :
        Description . . . . . . . . . . . : Realtek RTL8139 Family PCI Fast Ethe
rnet NIC
        Physical Address. . . . . . . . . : 00-40-05-7A-AA-40
        Dhcp Enabled. . . . . . . . . . . : Yes
        Autoconfiguration Enabled . . . . : Yes
        Autoconfiguration IP Address. . . : 169.254.227.178
        Subnet Mask . . . . . . . . . . . : 255.255.0.0
        Default Gateway . . . . . . . . . :

Ethernet adapter Wireless Network Connection 3:

        Connection-specific DNS Suffix  . :
        Description . . . . . . . . . . . : Instant Wireless USB Network Adapter
ver.2.6 #2
        Physical Address. . . . . . . . . : 00-06-25-19-96-49
        Dhcp Enabled. . . . . . . . . . . : Yes
        Autoconfiguration Enabled . . . . : Yes
        Autoconfiguration IP Address. . . : 169.254.186.233
        Subnet Mask . . . . . . . . . . . : 255.255.0.0
        Default Gateway . . . . . . . . . :

C:\Documents and Settings\EasySteps>_
```

Netstat

Netstat displays information about all the active connections on your computer.

Type netstat /? at the DOS prompt to list the command options.

```
Command Prompt                                                      _ □ ×

C:\Documents and Settings\EasySteps>netstat

Active Connections

  Proto  Local Address          Foreign Address        State
  TCP    Study:3033             pdb1.shop.vip.dcn.yahoo.com:http  ESTABLISHED
  TCP    Study:3037             phoneandwireless.com:http  ESTABLISHED
  TCP    Study:3039             img5.store.vip.sc5.yahoo.com:http  ESTABLISHED
  TCP    Study:3040             img5.store.vip.sc5.yahoo.com:http  ESTABLISHED
  TCP    Study:3025             localhost:microsoft-ds  TIME_WAIT
  TCP    Study:3029             localhost:microsoft-ds  TIME_WAIT
  TCP    Study:3030             localhost:microsoft-ds  TIME_WAIT
  TCP    Study:1055             169.254.44.127:netbios-ssn  TIME_WAIT

C:\Documents and Settings\EasySteps>_
```

Tracert

Tracert traces the route through the network to the destination computer or URL that you specify.

Type tracert at the DOS prompt to see the list of command options.

```
Command Prompt                                                      _ □ ×

C:\Documents and Settings\EasySteps>tracert www.google.com

Tracing route to www.google.com [216.239.39.99]
over a maximum of 30 hops:

  1     *        *        *        Request timed out.
  2   222 ms   239 ms   239 ms    renf-dam1-a-fa00.inet.ntl.com [62.252.129.193]
  3   238 ms   239 ms   239 ms    renf-t2core-a-pos43.inet.ntl.com [62.252.128.133]
  4   237 ms   239 ms   239 ms    ren-bb-a-so-200-0.inet.ntl.com [62.253.184.81]
  5   257 ms   259 ms   239 ms    bre-bb-b-so-200-0.inet.ntl.com [62.253.185.166]
  6   258 ms   259 ms   259 ms    win-bb-a-so-400-0.inet.ntl.com [213.105.172.233]
  7   257 ms   259 ms   260 ms    bcr2-so-7-0-0.London.cw.net [166.63.161.229]
  8   259 ms   259 ms   259 ms    bcr2-so-7-0-0.Thamesside.cw.net [166.63.209.205]
  9   337 ms   339 ms   339 ms    dcr2-loopback.Washington.cw.net [206.24.226.100]
 10   338 ms   339 ms   339 ms    bhr1-pos-10-0.Sterling1dc2.cw.net [206.24.238.16
6]
 11   338 ms   339 ms   339 ms    csr11-ve242.Sterling2dc3.cw.net [216.109.66.99]
 12   338 ms   339 ms   339 ms    218-google-exodusdc.exodus.net [216.109.88.218]
 13   338 ms   339 ms   339 ms    216.239.47.46
 14   337 ms   338 ms   339 ms    216.239.39.99

Trace complete.
```

You can specify the destination you want to trace either as an IP address, local name or URL.

Diagnostics Using MS Help and Support Center

The Microsoft Help and Support Center, accessible from the Start menu, includes a Network Diagnostics tool that will run a series of tests on your computer and its network connections and report back whether your system passes or fails each test.

Using the Network Diagnostics tool

1 Click Start, Help and Support, and under Pick a Task click Use Tools to view your computer information and diagnose problems.

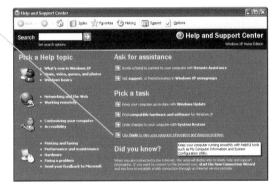

2 In the Tool pane on the left, click Network Diagnostics.

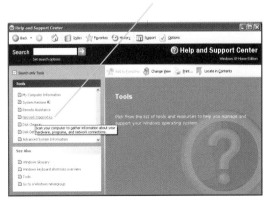

3 In the next dialog box you have two options, either to Set scanning options or to Scan your system.

Click Scan
your system

4 Network Diagnostics will scan your systems and report back a list of information gathered on each item tested.

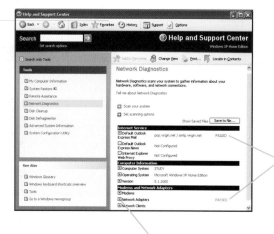

The list shows whether network components have passed or failed the diagnostic tests.

5 Click on the + button beside each element in the list to view further details of the diagnostic information gathered.

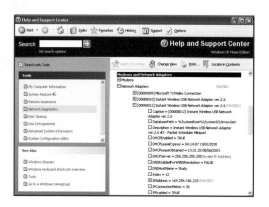

The Future of Networking

In this chapter we'll take a look at current and future developments in networking, particularly wireless networking, that seem likely to make it a pervasive technology in the home of the (not to distant) future.

We'll see how this technology looks set to revolutionize the way we interact with every electronic device in the home, from the fridge to the phone.

Covers

Chapter Eleven

What's in Store?

Future developments in networking are going to be most notable in the area of wireless, with new devices making wireless networks a commonplace throughout tomorrow's homes.

Linking home entertainment devices such as DVDs and Hi-Fi systems through a wireless home network is expected to drive a tripling of the number of installed home networks from the year 2002 to 2007.

Get ready for a pervasive home network...

Starting with home entertainment systems, the vision of the industry is of a home network branching out to provide connectivity for devices and systems that provide internal and external communications, maintain the in-home environment, ensure security as well as various housekeeping appliances.

...with total connectivity...

Major companies in the personal computer, mobile device and consumer electronics industries are working together in the Digital Home Working Group to set the standards that will allow digital content to be shared across a network linking all these types of devices. Wi-Fi will be the transport medium at the heart of these developments because of its flexibility and low cost.

...and more speed

As we've seen, a network packet carries a lot of protocol baggage as well as the actual data. With the overhead for encryption, error correction and traffic management, the actual user data rate of an 802.11g link will be around 20Mbps.

The IEEE's 802.11g standard, raising the headline data transmission rate to 54Mbps was approved in June 2003, and the next set of standards, which is likely to be designated 802.11n looks set to ramp up the speed to 108Mbps and possibly 320Mbps. Ratification of 802.11n is expected in 2006.

If you've just set up your first Wi-Fi home network, and are still excited about sending files over the airwaves at 11Mpbs, these speeds may seem unnecessary. The coming need for speed is based on the bandwidth required to stream video, for example from a DVD in the living room to the screen on a network-ready kitchen appliance.

Networked Media: Wi-Fi Meets Hi-Fi

Major companies like Sony (RoomLink) and Panasonic (AVC Server) are developing Digital Media Adapters or Network Players that act as a bridge for digital content between a PC, network-attached storage and a consumer electronics device such as a Hi-Fi system or TV.

Sony RoomLink

Until standards mature some of these devices may have proprietary interfaces. Sony's RoomLink for example only works with Sony PCs.

Network vendors Linksys and Netgear are also developing new devices to compete with Prismiq's MediaPlayer launched in 2003. Connecting to your stereo and TV allows you to:

- scan for available digital music, image and video files anywhere in your network,

- stream digital music, image and video to any available audio or video device in your home,

If your interest is in streaming music, then take a look at the cd3o network MP3 player at www.cp3o.com.

- retrieve play-list and program information from the Internet and play Internet radio on your stereo.

Controlling these devices will be a new breed of remote like the Philips iPronto, which will enable you to operate your entertainment systems, PC and surf the Internet all from one stylish handheld device.

Some of the early devices, based on 802.11b, are not supporting video streaming. This will become more common as the new 802.11g standard gets going.

Philips iPronto

Tomorrow's Phone: Wi-Fi + VoIP

As the name suggests, Voice over Internet Protocol (VoIP) is all about using the Internet as the underlying transport technology for voice messages.

These messages are traditionally person-to-person or phone-to-phone, but with a wider range of personal devices likely to be networked in the future, we will also see device-to-phone and PC-to-phone services.

Early VoIP experience was plagued by dropped packets, resulting in unintelligible conversations, but new technology and standards mean that VoIP is making a reappearance and is likely to be a major application of broadband Internet in the future.

New devices...
Network vendors Cisco together with Spectralink, Symbol and others are introducing devices to allow VoIP in wireless networks.

To run VoIP on your home network you need a special handset as well as a broadband Internet connection at both ends of the conversation. If your home network is wireless, the handset will allow you to roam around within the range of your access point.

Cisco IP 7920

Yep! You're right.
Looks just like a cell phone.

While traditional handset makers like Motorola are working on new handsets that will support both cellular and VoIP calls.

...supported by new standards
A key milestone will be ratification of IEEE 802.11e which provides a quality of service mechanism to ensure that voice data packets get priority when bandwidth becomes congested. This is needed to solve the dropped packets problem.

Another technical issue is enabling roaming between access points without dropping the call. Again the IEEE comes to the rescue, with the Inter Access Point Protocol (IAPP) included in the 802.11f standard which was completed in June 2003.

The Networked Home

Now that you've got your PCs networked, and perhaps the stereo and TV as well, it's time to start thinking about the other appliances around the home.

If you've really caught the networking bug there are plenty of companies out there network enabling everything from home security to the fridge.

Home security

Some wireless video cameras are known to cause interference on 2.4GHz Wi-Fi networks. Check compatibility.

For your first steps in networked home security try connecting a Wi-Fi enabled video camera, like the D-Link DCS-1000W.

You can set up this kind of camera with motion detection software that will record any movement and relay pictures over the Internet to allow you to keep an eye on your home when you're away.

You can find a helpful article about setting up the DCS-1000W on the Microsoft site at www.microsoft.com/ windowsxp/expertzone/columns.

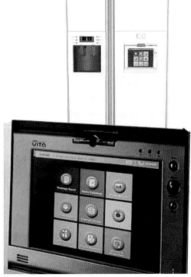

Home appliances

With a price tag of $8,000 when launched in 2003, it may well be a few years before this appears in many kitchens!

The Samsung HomePAD Internet Refrigerator may be typical of the kind of kitchen appliances that we'll all be buying in a few years time. Its removable HomePAD is a tablet PC that allows you to surf the Internet, view digital media, keep your recipes up to date and much more.

Portable screen displays

This type of removable display will likely become the PC access device of the future too, with vendors like Philips and Viewsonic already shipping wireless enabled detachable monitors like the Philips desXcape shown here.

These displays effectively allow you to carry your desktop computer around the home with you.

Other networked devices

Embedded wireless networking is likely to appear in a wide range of personal devices in the near future. Many laptop computers are already being shipped with embedded Wi-Fi adapters thanks to Intel's Centrino, and Wi-Fi enabled PDAs like Palm's Tungsten C which appeared in 2003.

And beyond the networked home

Outside, on the street, it won't be long before your car is hooked in to a wireless network too. Car makers and network solutions companies are already talking about enabling cars to connect to Wi-Fi access points at service stations.

You may also hear the term ad hoc or peer-to-peer in relation to mesh networks. "Ad hoc" refers to real-time changes in the network topology as stations move about, creating the need for adaptive routing software to enable these self-forming networks.

On the move we're back to the challenges of range and roaming between access points, but mesh technology may be the solution. In a mesh, each receiver also doubles up as a repeater station, and associations between these stations are established, ended and reestablished adaptively as stations move around.

There's no doubt the technology can be developed, the real question is whether the market for services like in-car video conferencing and video streaming is there to sustain the investment.

Networking Information Sources

Networking, particularly wireless networking, is a fast moving area with a wealth of information available online, from technical aspects of hardware and software, to information about organizing community wireless LAN projects.

Here you'll learn about some of the most useful websites to keep you up to date with the latest developments on the networking scene.

Covers

Chapter Twelve

General Networking

Sites listed here give general information to help with setting up home networks and background information on networking technology and new developments.

www.homenethelp.com

This is a site dedicated to helping home network users at the beginner and intermediate level.

www.homepcnetwork.com

Home PC Network provides practical coverage of everything related to Personal Computer networks.

Other home network information sites worth visiting:

- www.linuxhomenetworking.com
- www.homenetnews.com

Wireless Networking

See also the general networking sites, which cover an increasing range of wireless networking topics.

www.practicallynetworked.com

Practical help on wireless networking, with product reviews and step by step help.

www.pcworld.com

The wireless section contains news, reviews, how-tos and downloads on wireless networking.

The websites of the main wireless networking equipment vendors are worth checking out for general information:

- linksys.com, lucent.com, dlink.com, and see also
- www.openwlan.com

Hotspot Directories

As well as the www.wifinder.com site introduced in chapter 4, there are a number of other sites that will help you find out about hotspot availability in your area.

www.wififreespot.com

A listing of free hotspots around the world.

www.hotspotlist.com

A directory of US and International hotspots, although the international coverage has some way to go to catch up with wifinder.

Some of these new start-ups may not last long. If you get a broken link just try Google!

Other hotspot information sites worth checking out:

- www.wi-fizone.com
- www.hotspot-hotel.com
- www.zdnet.co.uk

Community Wireless

You'll find a lot of sites on the Internet covering community wireless networking. They'll give you a wealth of information about setting up your own community project and about many other wireless networking topics.

www.seattlewireless.net

Seattle Wireless is a not-for-profit group developing a wireless broadband community network in the Seattle area.

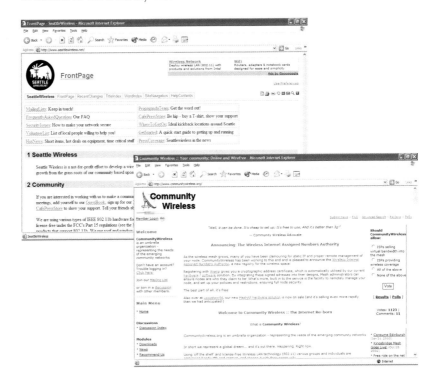

www.communitywireless.org

Community Wireless is an umbrella organization representing the needs of the emerging community networks.

Other community wireless sites worth a look include:

- www.freenetworks.org
- www.broadband-wireless.org and www.airshare.org

General Wireless Topics

A quick search on Google will reveal thousands of sites dedicated to all aspects of wireless computing and networking. Here are a few of the most useful.

www.wi-fiplanet.com

This is a complete guide to the world of 802.11 wireless, with news, reviews, features and tutorials.

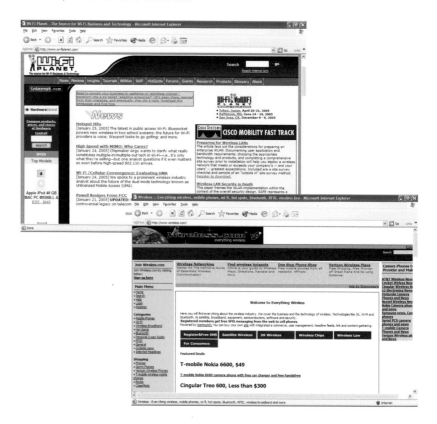

www.wireless.com

Wireless.com is a knowledge center on all things relating to wireless and mobile computing.

Other wireless information sites worth checking out include:

- www.dailywireless.org and www.wirelessweek.com
- www.wirelessinternet.com

Offbeat Wireless Topics

Wireless networking is a young and fast moving area of new technology that has not yet left its geeky origins completely behind. These offbeat sites give an insight into those origins.

www.wardriving.com

Their ongoing mission is to seek out new access points and unsecured wireless networks, and doing a good job of alerting us all to the security issues!

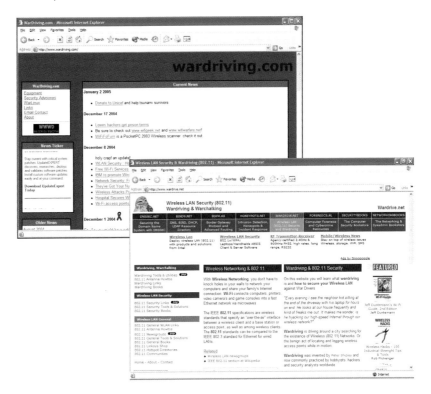

www.wardrive.net

Find out here all about wardriving, warchalking and what they mean for the security of your wireless network.

Here are a few others on a similar theme:

- www.warchalking.us and www.netstumbler.org
- www.homenetnews.com

Buying Networking Gear

You may end up at eBay or Amazon when you've decided what you want to buy. To get you to that point here are a few sites that will help you find the right equipment for your network.

www.pcmag.com

See PC Magazine and the sites of the other PC mags for product reviews of all the latest networking and wireless equipment.

www.epinions.com

You'll also find excellent hardware reviews and much more on this site, as well as at www.zdnet.com.

Other sites worth looking at before you buy your gear are:

- www.tigerdirect.com, www.outpost.com in the USA, and

- www.wlansource.co.uk, www.hotwireless.com in the UK.

Digital Home

Information about new products and other developments in the digital home of the future.

www.digitalhomemag.com

News, reviews and features on topics relating to the digital home of the future. It's got everything... including the kitchen sink!

www.yourdigitalhome.com

Featuring all the hardware components of the digital home, from automation and entertainment to security and communications.

Other digital home related sites worth taking a look at:

- www.pronto.philips.com
- www.hometoys.com and www.edgereview.com

Network Troubleshooting

The Microsoft Help and Support Center may be your first port of call for troubleshooting information, but there's a lot out there on the web too.

www.pcpitstop.com

A range of resources covering network troubleshooting under Windows and lots of other resources to keep your PC tuned-up.

www.annoyances.org

Information put together for and by Windows users. See the Troubleshooting articles for solutions to many networking problems.

And for the "official" view, try searching on home network troubleshooting on www.microsoft.com, as well as visiting www.homenethelp.com and www.practicallynetworked.com. See www.nakedwireless.ca for other helpful discussion forums.

Understanding the Specs

This chapter will give you a simple explanation of the key technical terms you will come across in the specifications of networking hardware and in other descriptions and discussions of networking, both wired and wireless.

Covers

Chapter Thirteen

Networking Alphabet Soup

Like all areas of Information Technology, networking would not be complete without its share of inscrutable acronyms. This easy guide covers the main terms you will encounter in setting up and working with your networking gear. A straightforward explanation of these terms can be found in the next section.

ACPI
Advanced Configuration and Power Interface

AFH
Adaptive Frequency Hopping

BPSK
Binary Phase Shift Keying

CCK
Complementary Code Keying

CSMA/CA
Carrier Sensing Media Access/Collision Avoidance

dBm
Decibels relative to 1 milliwatt power level

DBPSK
Differential Binary Phase Shift Keying

DFS
Dynamic Frequency Selection

DHCP
Dynamic Host Configuration Protocol

DQPSK
Differential Quadrature Phase Shift Keying

DSL
Digital Subscriber Line

DSSS
Direct Sequence Spread Spectrum

EIRP
Equivalent Isotropic Radiated Power

FHSS
Frequency Hopping Spread Spectrum

IP
Internet Protocol

IPSec
Internet Protocol Security

L2TP
Layer 2 Tunneling Protocol

MAC
Media Access Control

NAT
Network Address Translation

OFDM
Orthogonal Frequency Division Multiplexing

PBCC
Packet Binary Convolution Coding

PCMCIA
Personal Computer Memory Card International Association, or People Can't Memorize Computer Industry Acronyms!

PPTP
Point to Point Transport Protocol

QPSK
Quadrature Phase Shift Keying

SNMP
Simple Network Management Protocol

SSID
Service Set Identifier

TCP/IP
Transport Control Protocol / Internet Protocol

TKIP
Temporal Key Integrity Protocol

TPC
Transmitter Power Control

UDP
User Datagram Protocol

UTP
Unshielded Twisted Pair

VoIP
Voice over Internet Protocol

VPN
Virtual Private Network

WEP
Wired Equivalent Privacy

WOL
Wake-on-LAN

WPA
Wi-Fi Protected Access

If your inscrutable acronym is not in the list here, try internet.com's webopedia at www.webopedia.com.

What Does It All Mean?

Terms in **bold** type are defined elsewhere in this section.

802.11

The set of **IEEE** specifications that define wireless local area networks. 802.11b, also known as Wi-Fi, runs at up to 11Mbps on the 2.4GHz ISM radio band. Other 802.11 variants include 802.11a (up to 54Mbps in the 5GHz radio band) and 802.11g, ratified in June 2003, which uses the same 2.4GHz band as Wi-Fi, but also at data rates of up to 54Mbps.

10BaseT

The **IEEE** specification that uses **Unshielded Twisted Pair (UTP)** telephone cable for **Ethernet** connections running at 10Mbps. 10BaseF uses fiber optic cable instead of twisted pair cable, while 100BaseT and 1000BaseT variations run at 100Mbps and 1000Mbps.

A

Access Point

A wireless LAN transmitter/receiver that connects between wireless devices and wired networks. Depending on the manufacturer, an access point (AP) may provide features such as encryption, Internet connectivity via **DSL** or Cable and **DHCP** server functions, resulting in combined **Bridge**, **Router** and **Gateway** capabilities. An AP usually has connectors for one or more radio antennas, Internet (e.g. 56k modem, **DSL** or Cable modem), and a number of wired LAN devices.

Ad Hoc Mode

Also referred to as peer-to-peer mode or peer-to-peer networking, in ad hoc mode wireless enabled computers communicate with each other directly, without using an access point. See also **Infrastructure Mode.**

Adaptive Frequency Hopping (AFH)

A technique to allow **Bluetooth** and **Wi-Fi** devices, which both transmit on the 2.4GHz **ISM** band, to co-operate without interference. AFH limits the channels used by **frequency hopping** Bluetooth devices to avoid channels being used by **Wi-Fi** devices.

Advanced Configuration and Power Interface (ACPI)

ACPI gives the operating system more control over your computer for power management functions such as slowing down or going into sleep mode.

Asymmetric Digital Subscriber Line (ADSL)

One of a number of technologies that enables higher **bandwidth** over standard copper telephone lines. ADSL has a range of about 6km with data rates from home to Internet of 16 to 640Kbps and from Internet to home of 1.5 to 9Mbps.

B

Bandwidth

The total amount of data that can be transmitted in a certain period of time. Normally measured in megabits per second (Mbps) or kilobits per second (Kbps). For wireless communications it also refers to the amount of the frequency spectrum that is used for transmission.

Beamwidth

The angle of coverage provided by a radio antenna. A directional antenna decreases beamwidth and increases gain.

Binary Phase Shift Keying (BPSK)

A radio modulation technique, used by **802.11**b wireless devices at a data rate 1Mbps. BPSK uses two phases of the radio frequency carrier wave to represent 1s and 0s in the data stream.

Bluetooth

A wireless technology used for voice and data links over short ranges. Bluetooth uses the 2.4GHz radio band and has a range of around 10 meters, with a data rate of 720Kbps.

Bridge

A network component that provides connectivity between two networks, for example between wireless and wired networks. Windows XP can implement a network bridge in software when run on a computer that has connections to two networks.

C

Cardbus

A revised specification from the **PCMCIA** body that uses a 32-bit data bus and enables cards for Fast Ethernet at 100Mbps, compared to the initial 16-bit bus rate of 20Mbps. **PCMCIA** cards also became known as PC cards with the 1995 revision.

Carrier Sensing Media Access/Collision Avoidance

CSMA/CA is the method by which **Wi-Fi** transmitters avoid interfering with each other. A transmitter ready to send a data packet checks to see if another station is transmitting (Carrier Sensing). If another transmitter is detected it waits until the transmission ends. To ensure its data packet does not collide with a packet from another transmitter it then sends out a "Request to Send" signal to tell other stations it is about to transmit. If it gets a "Clear to Send" signal from the intended destination it transmits the data packet. If it hears another transmitter requesting air time it waits. And all that happens in a millisecond for every few hundred bits of transmitted data!

Complementary Code Keying (CCK)

A data encoding technique used in **Wi-Fi** networks for data transmission rates of 5.5 and 11Mbps. The complementary codes are a set of 64 specific bit patterns that are used to encode the data signal and make it easier for the receiver to pick out a weak signal against background interference. At lower data rates a simpler technique called a Barker sequence is used.

Crossover Cable

An **Ethernet** cable in which the twisted pairs are crossed over so that the transmit pins on one end connect to the receive pins on the other. This type of cable is used to directly connect like devices, such as a computer to a computer or a hub to a hub.

D

dBi

A logarithmic ratio commonly used to measure antenna gain relative to an isotropic antenna. The greater the dBi value, the higher the gain and as a consequence the narrower the angle of coverage. See **Beamwidth**.

dBm

A logarithmic ratio used to measure power levels relative to 1 milliwatt (mW). A power level of x dBm is ten to the power (x/10) milliwatts. So for example, 20dBm is 100mW.

Differential Binary Phase Shift Keying (DBPSK)

A variation on the **BPSK** modulation technique used in **Wi-Fi** transmitters at data rates of up to 1Mbps.

Differential Quadrature Phase Shift Keying (DQPSK)

A radio modulation technique used in **Wi-Fi** networks for transmitting at data rates of 2Mbps.

Digital Subscriber Line (DSL)

A class of high speed Internet connections offering data rates of up to 1.5Mbps. See also **ADSL**.

Directional Antenna

A type of antenna that concentrates transmitted power into a narrow beam, increasing range at the expense of reduced angular coverage. Types of directional antenna include yagi, patch and parabolic.

Direct Sequence Spread Spectrum (DSSS)

A **Spread Spectrum** data encoding technique that encodes each bit in the input data stream using a bit pattern called a chipping code. The longer the chipping code, the greater the chance that the input data can be recovered even if one or more bits are lost due to interference during transmission. Statistical techniques incorporated in the receiver circuit use the chipping code to recover the original data, minimizing the need for retransmission. See **CCK**, **FHSS**.

Diversity Antennas

An intelligent system that continuously senses the strength of incoming radio signals on two antennas and automatically selects the antenna receiving at maximum strength.

Dynamic Frequency Selection (DFS)

A supplement to the **802.11** standard to enable **WLAN**s operating in the 5GHz band to comply with European regulations. DFS selects the transmission channel to minimize interference with other users of the band, particular radar systems.

Dynamic Host Configuration Protocol (DHCP)

A protocol used in many operating systems, including Windows XP, that automatically issues network information such as an **IP address** to a device as it connects to the network. The device retains the assigned address for a specific administrator-defined period of time known as a lease.

Equivalent Isotropic Radiated Power (EIRP)

EIRP is the total effective transmitted power including gain from the antenna and any losses from cable and connectors. A 100 milliwatt (mW) transmitter with a 3dB antenna will transmit at an EIRP of 200 mW, excluding any losses in the system. EIRP limits are specified by the FCC in USA and the Radio Communications Agency (RCA) in UK.

Ethernet

The predominant wired Local Area Network (**LAN**) technology, standardized in the **IEEE** 802.3 specification. It provides data rates of up to 10Mbps. Fast Ethernet (100Mbps) and Gigabit Ethernet (1000Mbps) are higher speed variations.

Firewall

A software or hardware component that interfaces the network to the outside world and blocks certain types of traffic to avoid unauthorized access. Firewalls are an essential part of network security, but they require careful configuration to ensure correct operation and avoid unwanted interruption of valid network traffic.

Frequency Hopping Spread Spectrum (FHSS)

A **Spread Spectrum** technique, used in **Bluetooth** devices, that modulates the data signal with a carrier that hops from frequency to frequency as a function of time. A hopping code determines the sequence of frequencies used to transmit and the receiver uses the same code to change receiving frequency. See also **DSSS**, which is the method used for **Wi-Fi** transmission.

Fresnel Effect

A radio propagation phenomenon whereby an object that does not obstruct the direct visual line of sight obstructs the line of transmission for radio frequencies.

Gateway

A network component that connects to the Internet. The Internet connection may be of many different types, such as 56k modem, **DSL**, Cable Modem, etc. A gateway may also provide functions such as **DHCP**, **NAT** and **VPN**. See also **Router**.

Hub

A network device that connects centrally to other network devices, for example at the center of a star topology. A hub broadcasts each received data packet to every other device to which it is connected, so that available **Bandwidth** is shared between all networked devices. See **Switch**.

Infrastructure Mode

The wireless network configuration where communication between networked computers is via an access point rather than direct computer to computer. See **Ad Hoc Mode**.

Institute of Electrical and Electronics Engineers (IEEE)

The organization responsible for setting standards for wired networks or **Ethernet**.

Internet Protocol (IP)

The protocol that provides addressing and routing functions on the Internet.

Internet Protocol Security (IPSec)

An encryption method used in **VPN** networking that enables data sent between two computers to be encrypted and verified, even when using an insecure network such as the Internet.

IP Address

A binary number that uniquely identifies a host computer on the Internet so that other computers can address data packets to it.

ISM

The license exempt Industrial, Scientific and Medical radio band, at 2.4 to 2.483GHz. Divided into 13 channels in the UK, or 11 in the USA.

Level 2 Tunneling Protocol (L2TP)

A variation on **PPTP** that is used to manage secure **VPN** connections.

Line of Sight

An unobstructed line between a transmitter and receiver, as required for any long-range radio link in the **ISM** band. A Line of Sight Survey shows whether one aerial can be seen by another with no obstructions, such as buildings or trees, in the way.

Local Area Network (LAN)

A short-distance network used to link a group of computers and other devices such as printers over distances typically up to 500 meters. **10BaseT Ethernet** is the most common type of wired LAN and **802.11**b or **Wi-Fi** is the most common wireless LAN.

Media Access Control (MAC) Address

The unique hardware address of a network connection. For security reasons, some ISPs insist on knowing the MAC addresses of devices connecting to their system. On a wireless **LAN**, MAC address filtering can prevent unauthorized access by a device unless its MAC address is registered.

Modulation
The technique used to combine digital data with a transmitter's carrier signal.

Multipath Interference
The result of a primary signal combining with echo signals caused by reflections from objects on or near the line of sight between the transmitter and receiver. Reflected signals arrive at the receiver later than the primary signal and distort the received signal. Data encoding techniques such as **CCK** are used to make wireless links less sensitive to this type of interference.

Network Address Translation (NAT)
The translation of a local network addresses into an address that can be recognized by an Internet device. The translation is performed by **Gateway**s and **Router**s, and allows all devices on a **LAN** to share a single **IP Address**.

Omnidirectional Antenna (Omni)
An antenna with a 360 degree **Beamwidth**, used when transmission and reception is needed in all directions.

Orthogonal Frequency Division Multiplexing (OFDM)
An alternative to **DSSS** that provides higher data rates. Used in **802.11**a and **802.11**g wireless networking hardware to achieve data rates up to 54Mbps.

Packet Binary Convolution Coding (PBCC)
An alternative data coding and modulation scheme that allows **802.11** networks to operate at higher data rates. PBCC, developed by Texas Instruments, came a close second in the race

to be adopted as the basis of the **802.11**g standard, but tops out at 33Mbps compared to the 54Mbps achievable with **OFDM**.

PCMCIA (Personal Computer Memory Card International Association)

An industry association formed in 1989 to define standards for portable computer expansion cards. PCMCIA cards are now more commonly known as PC cards. See also **Cardbus**.

Point to Point Transport Protocol (PPTP)

A protocol that allows secure transmission of data over **Virtual Private Networks** (**VPN**) that make use of insecure network connections such as public telephone lines.

Protocol

A standard set or rule, or language, for communication between devices. **TCP** and **IP** are examples of protocols.

Quadrature Phase Shift keying (QPSK)

A radio modulation technique, used by **802.11**b wireless devices at data rates of 2Mbps and higher. QPSK uses four phase states of the carrier wave, each of which carries two bits of data from the input data stream.

Receiver Sensitivity

A measure of the weakest signal that a receiver can correctly decode into data. In wireless links using the **802.11**b standard the data communication rate is progressively reduced as the received signal weakens to give improved receiver sensitivity.

Router

A network device that transfers messages around the Internet by forwarding them to other routers or gateways. A router examines the **IP Addresses** within a data packet and forwards the packet on towards its destination. A key part of the router's function is to learn and share information about paths to other network destinations.

S

Service Set Identifier (SSID)

An identifier attached to data packets that functions as a password for a wireless network. Access points or other stations in a wireless network will ignore data packets that are not labeled with their SSID.

Simple Network Management Protocol (SNMP)

A communications protocol used by administrators to configure and monitor network nodes such as access points and gateways. Used to perform network management functions such as traffic monitoring and **MAC** filtering.

Spread Spectrum

A data encoding technique that spreads a radio signal over a wide band of frequencies. In this way the signal becomes less susceptible to noise and interference from other radio-based systems operating at similar frequencies. See **DSSS** and **FHSS**.

Switch

A network device, similar to a hub, but which actively switches data packets to the destination device.

T

Temporal Key Integrity Protocol (TKIP)

One element of the **WPA** security enhancement defined by the **IEEE** 802.11i standard that manages the sharing and changing of encryption keys between computers and access points.

Transport Control Protocol (TCP)

The basic communication language of the Internet and other networks. TCP manages the fragmentation of a message into packets that are transmitted individually over the Internet, and then manages the reconstruction of the original message from the received packets. It also handles error checking and retransmission of missing packets.

User Datagram Protocol (UDP)

A data transmission protocol that performs similar functions to **TCP**, but does not check for the arrival of all data packets or request retransmission of missing packets. Used for applications such as **VoIP** or video streaming, where late packets are simply ignored.

Uplink Port

A special port on a **hub** or **switch** which is intended to connect to another hub or switch in order to expand the network. If no uplink port is available the hub-to-hub or switch-to-switch connection can be made between standard ports using a **crossover cable**.

Unshielded Twisted Pair (UTP)

The most common type of cabling for wired **Ethernet** connections. The standard Ethernet cable consists of four twisted pairs terminated with RJ45 jacks.

Virtual Private Network (VPN)

A private data network that uses the public telecoms network but preserves privacy by encrypting data. The encryption/decryption process is managed by a "tunneling protocol" such as **IPSec**, **L2TP** or **PPTP**. Some **Wi-Fi** hotspot operators provide VPN tunneling to allow secure access to email.

Voice over Internet Protocol (VoIP)

The transmission of phone calls over the Internet. Uses the **UDP** transmission protocol. Mobile phones based on **Wi-Fi** and VoIP are reaching the market and may be a realistic alternative to 3G phones in areas where **Wi-Fi** roaming can be achieved.

Wake-on-LAN (WOL)
A feature that allows a network adapter to wake up the host computer from sleep mode so that resources attached to the host computer can be made available to other network users.

Wi-Fi Protected Access (WPA)
An update to **802.11** security specified in the 802.11i standard, which provides stronger encryption, manages network distribution of encryption keys, as well as user authentication and message integrity checking.

Wired Equivalent Privacy (WEP)
An optional feature of the **802.11** standard used to provide security equivalent to that of a wired **LAN**. WEP uses an encryption algorithm with a 40-bit or 60-bit key. When enabled, each computer and access point uses the shared key to encode data before transmission. Any received data packet that is not properly encoded is discarded. See **WPA**.

Wireless Ethernet Compatibility Alliance (WECA)
Sponsors of the **Wi-Fi** standard, which assures interoperability of **802.11**b wireless networking components.

Wireless Fidelity (Wi-Fi)
The standard as specified by **WECA** that ensures the interoperability of wireless networking components designed according to the **IEEE 802.11**b standard. The Wi-Fi logo on wireless networking products gives a guarantee of interoperability.

Wireless Internet Service Provider (WISP)
A provider of public Internet access via wireless network links.

Wireless Local Area Network (WLAN)
A local area network that transmits data using unlicensed radio frequencies such as the 2.4GHz **ISM** band. Wireless access points may be connected to an **Ethernet** hub or server and transmit radio signals over distances of several hundred meters.

Index

D

E

F

G

H